+JC330 .K437 1991

```
JC      Khoshkish, A.
330
.K437    Power or
1991    authority?
```

	DATE DUE	

AUDREY COHEN COLLEGE LIBRARY
345 HUDSON STREET
NEW YORK, NY 10014

POWER OR AUTHORITY?
THE ENTELECHY OF POWER

A. Khoshkish

UNIVERSITY
PRESS OF
AMERICA

Lanham • New York • London

Copyright © 1991 by A. Khoshkish
University Press of America®, Inc.
4720 Boston Way
Lanham, Maryland 20706

3 Henrietta Street
London WC2E 8LU England

All rights reserved
Printed in the United States of America
British Cataloging in Publication Information Available

Library of Congress Cataloging-in-Publication Data
Khoshkish, A.
Power or authority/ : the entelechy of power / A. Khoshkish.
  p.   cm.
Includes bibliographical references and index.
1. Power (Social sciences) 2. Authority. I. Title.
JC330.K437 1991 303.3' 3—dc20 91-24844 CIP

ISBN 0-8191-8395-4 (alk. paper)

 The paper used in this publication meets the minimum requirements of American National Standard for Information Sciences—Permanence of Paper for Printed Library Materials, ANSI Z39.48–1984.

To Irene

CONTENTS

Preface	vii-ix
I. Introduction	1
II. Domination Drive	7
III. Types of Power Relationships	13
■ Catatonic	14
■ Commensal	17
■ Symbiotic	22
■ Divergent	24
■ Conflicting	25
IV. The Nature of the Product of Power Relationships	29
■ Product-Cost Replenishment Functions	29
■ Potentio-Kinetic Convertibility	31
V. Sources of Power	35
■ Brute Force	36
■ Means	39
■ Position	41
■ Connection	42
■ Power of Persuasion and Influence	44
■ Self-Confidence, Charisma and Reputation	46
■ Consciousness and Will	49
VI. Coefficients of Power	57

VII. Spheres of Power	65
VIII. Resistants of Power	83
IX. From Power to Law and Authority	91
▪ Temporal and Coexistential Phenomena	91
▪ Natural, Rational and Normal Behavior	94
▪ Legitimization Processes	97
▪ Justification = Justice	99
X. Conclusion	107
Selected Bibliography	109
Index	125

PREFACE

The antecedents of this inquiry go back to the late 1960's when a need was felt to examine power in itself in contrast to the then prevailing game theory and behavioral approaches to power (notably by Harsanyi, Dahl, March, Gamson, Bachrach and Baratz). The results of that study were presented to the Midwest Political Science Association in Chicago in 1971 under the title of "The Concept of Power: A Potentio-Kinetic Approach". Many of the ideas developed then have since become common concern in political philosophy and covered by many authors, permitting us to re-evaluate and document some of those ideas.

But the trend in the past two decades has become more and more normative (Lukes, Martin, Morriss, Isaac), -- some remaining descriptive (Nagel, Oppenheim) -- with confining results. The reinjection of the phenomenological dimension into the formal, descriptive and normative treatments of power seemed again justifiable in order to keep our perspectives open.

The results of the revisit to the topic were reported to the International Political Science Association's Study Group on Political Power in London in 1989. The present monograph is a reedited version of that report and is prepared in proper printed form for the use of colleagues and students who have expressed interest in our approach.

A word on the "we" authorship of this monograph. A colleague inquired whether it implied co-authorship or, adding facetiously, it was the royal "we"! The answer was that it represented the traditional method used by authors who know that what they expound is the outcome of their interaction with their total environment. The alpha of this monograph's authorship is lost in time and space, somewhere between the Greek philosophers and the legalists of China, and its omega is Jacques Havet, respected friend and colleague of old, whose incisive comments on the last version of the manuscript greatly contributed to its improvement. To him and all go "our" thanks. But a book is a living being. It communicates with the reader and the "we" becomes the communion of the two. That communion is essential for our understanding. Power cannot be grasped as a string of elements but as a complex of thought. At all moments of our discourse its whole is present. Yet, because of the limitations of the written word all does not exude at once. That is the handicap of the writer compared to a painter who can unveil the canvas once completed. The writer has to beg for patience for the ideas that are yet to come and remind the reader of the thoughts that have flown by.

The more obvious factor of the total environment affecting our study is, of course, the literature quoted or listed in our selected bibliography. While our search and research have been greatly influenced by the works listed in the selected bibliography we have not always had the occasion to quote them in the text. The purpose of this short essay is not to review the literature referred to or mentioned in the bibliography. We have our own approach to deal with and assume that those who get involved are either familiar with the literature or our mention of it will whet their appetite to seek it.

Preface

Although the tone and tenure of this monograph is academic, if the practitioners of power cared to plough through it, they may find it not without practical interest. Philosophical discourse on power can provide food for thought for fathers, corporate executives, presidents, governors, and dictators who are concerned about the control of their domains. Whether it is the imperative of shifting weight within their spheres of power to remain on top or the need to perceive and evaluate resistants within their power complex, they can draw inspiration from abstract concepts for developing concrete strategies.

This revision has been undertaken during a period ripe with significant events, from the advent of perestroika in the Soviet Union and the unification of Germany, to the crises in the Middle East. Where appropriate, we have used historical examples for our concepts. The temptation to illustrate them by current events was great and we indulged several times. But succumbing to that temptation altogether would have made us chase those events and never finish the monograph. Rather, it would be more interesting for the readers to test the ideas developed in this essay against current events; whether it is, as these lines are being written, our concept of Domination Drive against Boris Yeltsin's bent for leadership, our analysis of the Spheres of Power against the dynamics of glasnost and perestroika or the German unification, or whatever the phenomena of the time may be. The test will permit the reader to mend and amend whatever is lacking in our understanding of power.

A. Khoshkish

New York City, May 1991.

I

INTRODUCTION

> *There was power long before there was a written word for it.*
>
> *- Charles E. Merriam*

This is an inquiry into the phenomenon of power: An attempt to examine power as it is in itself.[1] As Merriam's words emphasize, power is not confined to human terms of reference. In that spirit, we intend to extend our inquiry to the limits of our perception and yet recognize that power cannot be circumscribed within those limits. Thus, our approach will take us beyond the strict study of power within the human societal context. True, as Dahl says, we shall have our hands full if we confine our study to the power relationship between human beings.[2] But keeping our hands full

---

1. The phenomenology used is crudely Husserlian, *i.e.*, an attempt to consider power as it is in itself, in transcendental sphere, on the basis of original intuition drawn from primordial phenomena through methodic procedure. Husserl, 1929, 1931. As we shall see, a study of power in itself does not necessarily imply a non-causal essence independent of power's relational existence. On the causal nature of power see Nagel, 1975.

2. Dahl, 1957, p.203.

with the human dimensions of power for too long may narrow our perspective. Indeed, following Dahl's advice, recent studies of power have focused on its social aspects and immersed it in normative systems and begun confusing it with ideology and authority.[3] Surely law, authority and normative systems contain considerable elements of power and vice-versa. But confusing them muddles the issue.

We can better realize the dichotomy by moving to the confines of human affairs. A student of international relations, for example, is more sensitive to the phenomenon of power in itself beyond its convolution in normative systems. From an international perspective, normative systems, *i.e.*, beliefs and ideologies, are more distinctly identifiable as persuasion components for the legitimization of power within autonomous complexes such as nations and states and are not confused with power.[4] In the international arena, norms of international law are often respected by powers which may not have common value systems. Beyond the two possible dimensions of conquest and defeat, superior and inferior, or power politics between entities which do not recognize each other's superiority or dominance and yet cannot overrun and absorb each other, powers create the third dimension of international norms to regulate their clashes and cooperation and to make the exer-

---

3.   Even in his treatment of the dichotomy of power and authority, Lukes eventually falls back on the Weberian intertwining of power and authority and reaffirms his own three dimensional view based on political agenda, latent social conflict, subjective and real interests and institutionalized power. Lukes, 1978, pp.662-669. For a critique of Lukes see Gray, 1980.

4.   On the persuasive dimension of authority see our later discussion of the conversion of power into authority.

I. Introduction

cise of their power reasonably predictable.[5] "Raw" power eventually creates norms and values for its own security and survival. But we are getting ahead of ourselves.

By avoiding a total immersion in the societal context we may find premises which we could use to explain and overcome normative constraints. Accordingly, while perforce the thrust of our inquiry will also be human affairs, in order not to get too entangled in the ideological, legal and normative envelopes, should our analogies of social and natural phenomena coincide, in our search for perspective, we shall permit ourselves some digression. Our purpose in doing so will be, to borrow Bertrand Russell's words, *"to suggest and to illuminate, but not to demonstrate"*.[6] That may give our essay an exotic flavor. For that, we beg for the readers' forgiveness and appeal to their imagination.[7]

The term entelechy in the title of this monograph has been borrowed from the Aristotelian theory of actualization of potentials.[8] It has a dynamic and fermenting connotation. In strict

---

5. For treatments of power at the international level see, for example, Aron, 1964; Ash, 1951; Baldwin, 1979; Cline, 1975; Morgenthau, 1967; Schelling 1963.

6. Russell, 1938, ch. XI.

7. Trogu, 1974, pp.9-10. See also his distinction between imperative and normative powers.

8. Notably, Aristotle, *Metaphysics*, IX, 3, 1047a and 8, 1050a (1968) pp. 438, (30-31) and 438 (24). These references are to the Greek text, as in the English translations of the collected works of Aristotle the term entelechy has been translated as potency (1908), potentiality (1968) and actuality (1984). Neither actuality nor potentiality, or potency, satisfy the purposes of our study. Initiation into the entelechy of power is crucial to decision-making. In the Gulf War, for example, had Saddam Hussein known what it takes to make the United States convert her potential power into actual power, he may

physical terms, potential is that which has not yet turned into kinetic energy, and kinetic is that which by its motion has ceased to be potential energy. The kinetic stopped in its course becomes the potential of its remaining energy. In other words, while on its course the kinetic energy carries with it the potentials of its continuity.

Potential and kinetic energies are relative in their probability. Max Planck always remembered how his high school teacher Mr. Müller had told them about the conservation of energy:

"He told us of the strength and power which a bricklayer needs to lift a huge stone to the roof of a building. The energy

---

have avoided the challenge to his power. As intimated by General Norman Schwarzkopf, commander of the Allied forces during the Gulf War, had Iraq occupied only the contested areas of Rumaila and the island of Bubiyan, the United States would have had a hard time mobilizing an army of half a million and mustering a coalition to face the army of Saddam Hussein in northern Kuwait. Entelechy is the understanding of the potentiality/actuality flux. It is its nuance that makes it the proper terminology for our approach. See also Blair, 1967. The Webster New Collegiate Dictionary (1977) defines entelechy as "the realization of form-giving cause as contrasted with potential existence". Because entelechy, as a word, is not in common use, and even less is "entelechic" as an adjective, we will often use potentio-kinetic instead.

Terminology itself can, of course, be *the* approach to the study of power. Indeed, although that approach is beyond the purview of our study, we cannot escape its confines. It is our hope, however, that the reader will surmount the confinement of the terms in order to get to the essential concepts we wish to convey. To paraphrase Wittgenstein, our propositions are elucidating insofar as whoever understands them, going through, over and above them, recognizes them as non-sensical and ascends beyond them (1921, 6.54). Or, put differently, we hope that each of our terms contains within it the seeds of its own destruction and as it dehisces in the reader's mind it gains its proper conceptual fertility (see Derrida, 1967, 1974).

I. Introduction

is never lost. It remains stored up, possibly for years, latent in the block of stone - until one day it is somehow loosened and, perhaps, drops on the head of some passerby".[9]

Of course the brick that is embedded in a solid wall, although a potential head-breaker, presents less danger than a brick which sits precariously on the edge of the wall.

The potentio-kinetic concept hinges on convertibility. The potential side of the potentio-kinetic concept of power corresponds to the Hobbesian definition: *"The Power of a Man, (to take it Universally,) is his present means, to obtain some future apparent good".*[10] But it is power insofar as the relationship between the present means and the future good is a dynamic, materializable reality. This qualification of Hobbes' definition is different from Parsons' paraphrase to the effect that *"--such means constitute his (the Hobbesian Man's) power, so far as these means are dependent on his relations to other actor".*[11] The two qualifications, the dependence of power on a relationship and its dynamic materialization, complement each other. It is in this existential and relational continuum that we propose to examine the concept of power.[12]

---

9. Quoted in Untermeyer, 1955, p. 270.

10. Hobbes, 1651, ch.X, para. 41.

11. Parsons, 1951, p. 121.

12. In the empirical and formal treatment of power within the societal and interpersonal context many researchers have pointed out the problems involved in the global treatment of potential and factual power. See notably Dahl, 1961, 1963, 1970; Harsanyi, 1962, a and b; Polsby, 1963; Nagel, 1968; Gamson, 1968; Wrong, 1979.

But first let us see why and how man comes to perceive the phenomenon of power. For that we need to begin with the examination of the early manifestations of the phenomenon within the psyche and its role as the cue for the identification of the self in its total environment.

II

DOMINATION DRIVE

At the very beginning of its existence, with its heavy brain and yet its weak body to carry it, the child encounters the realities of its contradictory being. Once out of the uterus it finally finds space to stretch and is, in a sense, freed from the confinement of the womb.[13] The fetus receives its oxygen, food and warmth in the mother's womb, but is limited in its movements. Having found space at birth, the child soon experiences the discomfort of hunger and changing temperature. It is at the mercy of its parents' care for the satisfaction of its basic needs and has to submit to their rhythm. When it is hungry or uncomfortable, it cries. Its crying, which may be beneficial for its growth if the needs causing it were satisfied within reasonable biological limits, can turn into rage if frustrated. Each of these possibilities and the spectrum of other variations between them will have effects on the development of the individual's character and personality.

---

13. Some psycho-biological experiments have demonstrated that the brain is capable of registering sensations *in utero*. We may thus infer that the fetus can sense the space limitation when it starts kicking the uterine wall. It has been shown, for example, that the fetus is capable of learning *in utero*. Spelt, 1948. Attempts have been made to demonstrate biological grounds for the domination drive. Hendrick, 1943 and White, 1959.

Soon the individual becomes conscious of his[14] dependence on his parents.[15] His dependence infringes upon his freedom and imposes restrictions on him. At the same time he becomes habituated to the care he receives and develops an expectation for attention. The degree of attention received and expected will differ from family to family and from culture to culture. The child's expectation of attention goes beyond the satisfaction of his biological needs and relates to his needs for affectional relationships and contact comfort.[16] This affectional attraction to the immediate environment, like the attraction for the satisfaction of biological needs, may meet a varying range of responses. But even under the most favorable circumstances the response cannot provide total fulfillment for the affectional needs. To mention but one obstacle, the need for affection and attention and the response for its fulfillment reside in different individuals. Even a dedicated and loving mother cannot meet her child's expectations of attention *ex toto et tempore*, simply because expectations will evolve in relation to their satiation.[17]

---

14. The terms "he", "his", "him", and "man" are used generically in this essay and where applicable refer to both female and male genders.

15. May, 1972, p. 20 and Part I, 5, *passim*. This statement does not necessarily contradict the point made by Eric Fromm about the unawareness of the child of his individuality at the beginning (Fromm, 1941). We are considering dependence and the consciousness of lacks rather than the consciousness of individuality. Our observation coincides, rather, with the Hegelian concept of generational dialectics. Hegel, (1821) 1967.

16. For experiments on contact comfort as animal drive see Harlow and Zimmermann, 1959.

17. On other approaches to the egocentric nature of the child -- and man -- see Le Dantec, 1918; and Piaget, 1967, IV §6 & V, as well as the latter's earlier writings.

II. Domination Drive

Thus the being, from the moment his brain becomes capable of registering his experiences to the moment when he becomes conscious of himself as an individual, is constantly confronted with situations presenting limitations and possibilities. On the one hand they attract him by the security they offer; on the other hand they repulse him by the dependence they impose upon him. Attraction-repulsion, love-hate, and the desire for freedom-security are, psychologically speaking, understandable in their togetherness and mutual presence. It is the degree of intensity of one in relation to the other in a given situation that influences the attitude of the individual and makes him, for example, consider enclosure as either contributing to his security or confining his freedom. Thus, all through life man has to make choices between alternatives. By the very nature of things he cannot have his cake and eat it too.

As the individual goes through different experiences in his life, first in his relations with his parents, then with his peers and his teachers, later with his colleagues and other members of the society, his dependence for security, freedom of action and opportunities is shifted to different sources. Of course, the optimum goal for him will be the possibility to control the sources on which he depends for his security, thus giving him freedom in their use and consequently "independence" from them. In its more complex form security here includes not only the fulfillment of physiological needs but also the satisfaction of all of man's drives, such as affectional relationships which, while including the attention of those who supply him with his physiological needs, can also become more abstract and cover such expectations as recognition, admiration and respect. In other words, all put together the individual wants to be on top of the situation and dominate it. The child who cries for food to draw the attention of those who care for him and finally receives satisfaction, or who later charms his mother to buy him the candy he wants, already has some control over the sources of his satisfaction.

The drive for domination, whether at the level of child-parent relationships or in the arena of social and political struggle broadly follows the Darwinian law of the survival of the fittest, or in the present context, the dominant position of the fittest. The domination drive will, of course, be subject to other variables within the social complex. There will be neutralizing and propelling factors influencing the individual drives. The dominant position will not necessarily be occupied by those with the highest raw domination drive quotient, but by those who reach the power position in the flux of social dynamics and fermentations. Thus, in the omnipresent drive for domination, some will settle for more and some will have to, or simply will, settle for less. Those who do settle for less extrinsically (rather than going for the challenge of control and freedom of action) have, intrinsically (in their motivated behavior) opted for what they may have perceived as the path of least friction, or security provided for them by the powerful -- for fear of the unknown.[18]

In the evolution of a power relationship, however, the dependence of those who have settled for less on those who dominate may eventually reduce the security the former originally sought. The goals of those who seek power for their own security and freedom, and who take control will not always coincide with the goals of those whom they dominate. In the extreme, the powerholders may develop a taste for power as an end in itself. It

---
18. Fromm, 1941; Lane 1959.

II. Domination Drive

will be sought not only to provide security and freedom, but to give its holder the pleasure of overcoming resistance and making others do what they would not have done otherwise. Its exercise will be its confirmation and a source of satisfaction for other drives such as the drives for excitement, game and challenge. Power may become engaged in a spiral of expansion.[19] Thus, depending on the circumstances, we may detect different degrees of harmony, compliance, resistance and conflict in power relationships.

---

19.   Adorno, 1950; Karlsson, 1962.

III

TYPES OF POWER RELATIONSHIPS

To explore these variations, let us schematize a little. Let A and B be power complexes in a power relationship.[20] Let us assume that when A wants B to act in a particular way (which we will designate in each case as i', j', k') it takes a particular action (which we will designate in each corresponding case as i, j, k). So, A performs i in order to make B perform i'. Formally this is expressed as $(Ai|Bi')$. The two variables may combine in different ways, depending on the nature of the relationship between A and B and their actions, as will be discussed in the following pages.

Under different circumstances the combination may be that of simple mathematical operations of addition or subtraction, more complicated calculus of vector functions, or even scalar quan-

---

20. We use "power complex" in order to avoid the term "actor", because "actor" tends to individualize the concept of power which we wish to keep abstract at this stage. By using the term "complex," we are emphasizing the complexity of the phenomenon whose whole is not always the sum of its parts. For us A represents power; it is not, even in human terms, an individual but that dimension of him which is power. So, when we later discuss A as landlord or the man on top of the wall, we refer to them insofar as they can actualize their power. The term "complex" can thus refer to a component of the power relationship, or to the relationship itself.

tifications more appropriate for the measurement of mass and energy. The relationship will render a "product" which we will designate as p; formally $(Ai|Bi') \longrightarrow p$.[21] The magnitude of p will, of course, depend on the nature of the relationship and interaction between A and B. The power relationship in a power complex matrix (which we will represent here for the power of A over B as $P(A/B)$ may oscillate between 1 and 0. That is to say, A's power over B will tend towards full power 1 when every time A does i, j, k, B does the corresponding i', j', k'. The power of A over B will tend towards 0 if every i, j, k action on A's part encounters non-compliance or resistance on the part of B, which we can represent as $\bar{i}', \bar{j}', \bar{k}'$. In between, where there is both compliance and resistance (as is usually the case), B's response will represent the net result depending on which is greater.

CATATONIC POWER RELATIONSHIP

Let us first conceive of an extreme situation where the dominated element is catatonic, *i.e.*, it presents insignificant resistance. It complies not because it finds that compliance corresponds to its goal, but because it has no vigor for self-actualization. In psychopathology, catatonic schizophrenia in some cases refers to what is called waxy flexibility, where the patient can be molded into different postures by others and keeps those postures for a long time.

---

21. We use "product" represented by the letter "p" where other authors have used the term "outcome." Notably March, 1957; Goldman, 1972. Our purpose is to symbolically underscore the relationship between the end product of a power relationship with that power relationship as a whole -- which we will represent by P.

III. Types of Power Relationships

In the catatonic situation, illustrated in Figure 1, B's resistance to A's action i tends toward 0 and A's power over B approaches 1 -- formally, $Bi' \longrightarrow 0$ and $P(A/B) \longrightarrow 1$.[22]

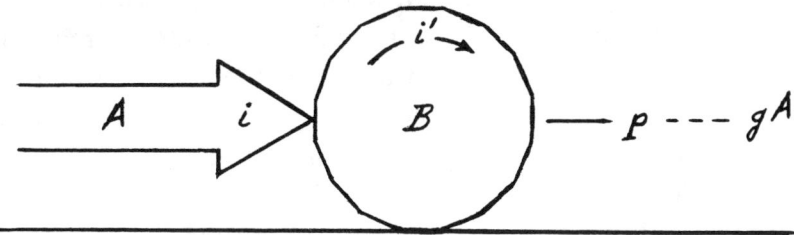

Figure 1

While A's power relationship with B approaches the total unit, the "product" of this power relationship may be 0 for A, because the amount of resources A will have to employ (which will be identical with A's action i in the catatonic situation) to make B perform i' may be nearly equal to i'; formally $i'/i \longrightarrow 1$, or $i\text{-}i' \longrightarrow 0$.

Although the product of the power relationship of A and B may[23] tend to zero, we may still consider A as more powerful than

---

22. In this catatonic hypothesis, resistance due to inertia is abstracted from Bi'. Also, for conceptual simplification, any resistance, whether willful or due to inertia, will be considered simply as resistance and dealt with as such in later models in this section.

23. The term "may" should be underscored here because $i'/i \to 1$ or $i\text{-}i' \to 0$ does not necessarily imply $p \to 0$. As we shall see later, relations and correlations in the power complex are not mechanical. Take, in the catatonic model, the example of A pushing B out of a hideout to exhaust enemy fire. A may have used kinetic energy equal to the movement of B, but the product may result in life for A and death for B. See our later discussion on the nature of the product "p" and its relation to A's goal in Ch.IV.

B if the proportion of A's total power potentials to its action i is bigger than B's total potentials compared to its action i'; formally, $A/i > B/i'$. In the long run if A uses a proportionally smaller amount of its resources for actions i, j, k than B does to perform its corresponding actions i', j', k' (assuming the same catatonic relationship continues), A will not simply maintain, but increase the ratio of its potentialities over B. This concept of proportionality will be more obvious in the other kinds of relationships discussed later.

If B's resistance became zero, B would cease as an independent power and would be considered a component of A -- or its extension. The mention of this extreme, which can be applied to human behavior only in rare psychopathological cases and, with qualification, to highly conditioned totemic subjects, calls for our awareness of such important characteristics of power as will and consciousness. These characteristics, which we shall discuss later, imply at this stage of our study that while B may be catatonic, A should have a goal g in making B perform i'. $(Ai|Bi')$ will render the product "p", which may or may not be identical with A's goal g. Also, p may or may not be lucrative for A. As an illustration of the non-lucrative case, take the extreme of power for the sake of power, which was mentioned earlier. Where A is a willful and conscious power, a catatonic power relationship will not be much of a confirmation for A's power and satisfaction, unless we combine a megalomaniac with a schizophrenic. In that case, A's exercise of power over B will be like kicking stones on the road. In game theory language, our catatonic situation will approach the so-called St. Petersburg Paradox, i.e., a one-person game where one tosses a coin until he wins.[24]

----
24.   Rapoport and Orwant, 1962, pp. 1-2.

III. Types of Power Relationships

If A's goal is lucrative, it is assumed that in the catatonic situation the product, if any, will totally accrue to A, formally $(Ai|Bi') \longrightarrow pA$. Of course, we can conceive of a situation where A may induce B to perform i' with part or all of the product p accruing to B. Take, for example, the case of the catatonic schizophrenia given as an illustration earlier. A may be the doctor's power creating some will in B, in which case because the result p accrues to B, A will have less and less of a catatonic relationship with B, and their relationship may evolve into one of the other situations described below. If A's power over B is to continue in one way or another, the product of their power relationship should be distributed so that a bigger part of it accrues to A's power potentials. For example, in our last illustration, while B gains more will-power by the doctor's Ai, he may at the same time gain more conscious respect for the doctor's power. Thus, $(Ai|Bi') \longrightarrow pA > pB$.

COMMENSAL POWER RELATIONSHIP

"Commensal" was the term used by Hawley to indicate the relationship between like species in their parallel efforts to make similar demands on their environment.[25] Its literal meaning is: "eating from the same table." In our concept of power, a commensal relationship resembles Harsanyi's model where A can make B move from an initial strategy to a second one more favorable to A.[26] Here Harsanyi's assumptions are implied. Let us say that landowner A does action i, which in our model can include canalization for ir-

---

25. Hawley, 1950.

26. Harsanyi, 1962a. We are not repeating Harsanyi's formal symbols here in order to avoid confusion with ours.

rigation and land improvement, favorable lease terms (Harsanyi's reward), and competitive pressure (Harsanyi's threat) to induce farmer B to leave his present low yield farm (Harsanyi's strategy one) to come and farm on A's land (Harsanyi's strategy two). B's coming onto A's farm is represented by i'.[27]

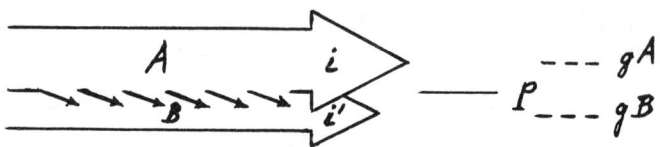

Figure 2

The power relationship of the landowner and the farmer is commensal in that they have a common goal -- in the elementary sense, their need to eat. Of course, the farmer B can farm his low yield land and the landowner A may have to farm his land himself instead of leasing it out. In such case there will be no commensal power relationship between A and B. There may be other power

---

27.	Thus in Harsanyi's terms, movement from first strategy to the second one. Symbols are simplified here because our purpose is to conceptualize rather than formalize power. With our present tools and methods of analysis we are better off dealing with the components of power relationships globally and leaving the breakdown into details for the examination of each particular case. As we shall see in our example of landowner-farmer relationship, Ai or the landowner's action should be analyzed in more terms than just reward and threat.

III. Types of Power Relationships

relationships between the two which could fall into one of the categories that follow. By engaging in a commensal power relationship they increase their chances for a better crop (Figure 2).

The product of their commensal power relationship may not be identical with the goals gA and gB which each of the powers A and B expect out of the relationship. Landowner A may have planned on benefits providing him funds for the expansion of the farm, while B may have counted on savings which would enable him to procure a fertile farm of his own. Each one's goal may handicap the other and in their compromise they may not reach their original goals. The relationship may thus have, in Harsanyi's terms, utilities and disutilities for both partners and finally yield product p. Of course, the power relationship is commensal in so far as A and B have the primary common goal of nourishing themselves. The more there are interests in their individual goals which are not compatible with those of the other, the more our model will tend to approach the divergent or conflicting power relationships explained below.

*   *   *

Before proceeding to other categories of power relationships, let us retain some aspects of this second model which will be useful for our later discussions. In general, as a result of A's action i, B will perform i'. Notice, however, that landowner A's action i included not only reward and threat directly addressed to B, but also land improvement and irrigation canalization, which are for A's general welfare too. One might say that these last items are independent of the power complex under consideration. But they surely did influence B's evaluation and final movement towards performing i'.

Let us make the point by another illustration. Suppose A is an excellent marksman and while he is performing i, that is, is target shooting, he is observed by B. Now, suppose he asks B to perform i' and B, having been impressed by A's marksmanship and assuming the threat of A's gun, complies. Yet, A may be a peaceful character who loves target shooting as a sport but would not think of using his gun on a living being.[28] We will leave B's subjective evaluation of A's intentions and A's consciousness of his power for a later stage of our discussion. At present what is to be retained is that A's action i which made B do i' was not directed to B. Of course, a range of situations may be conceived where A may do i partly addressed to B and partly for other purposes. A may have been shooting in our example not only for practice and fun, but also to impress B. A military parade is simultaneously a festivity and a demonstration of force to evoke pride in the citizens, to assure the allies and to threaten the enemies.

While the consideration of all of Ai will be useful for the understanding of B's subjective evaluation of its power relationship with A, only that part of i which has been exerted or spent by A directly to bring about Bi' should be taken into account for the assessment of A's costs. This cost, as we said earlier, can include expenses other than direct reward and threat addressed to B.[29] We can represent this cost by i_c and complement the formula presented in the case of a catatonic power relationship accordingly:

---

28. See, notably, Luce and Adams, 1956, on the misperception of other parties' aims.

29. On cost see Goldman, 1972, and Barry's treatment of "costs of carrying out promises ...and threats", in Barry, 1976.

III. Types of Power Relationships

$$i' > i_c, \ A/i_c > B/i', \ p > 0, \ (Ai \,|\, Bi') \longrightarrow pA > pB$$

This, of course, is a clear-cut and straight-forward potentio-kinetic power position for A. Because A's cost is less than B's efforts, the proportion of A's cost to its resources is smaller than that of the ratio between B's efforts and resources, and a bigger portion of the end product accrues to A. Situations may arise, however, where one or more of the favorable conditions may not exist and yet A may still be considered to have power over B. Take for example the case where A may have had costs greater than B's efforts, or the ratio of A's costs and resources was smaller than that of B's, but that the amount of p accrued to A was of such a magnitude that it compensated for the other unfavorable conditions. Or take the case where the ratio of A's costs and resources was so insignificant that although a bigger part of the product accrued to B, all in all A came out of the deal more powerful. Although, as we shall see later in our discussion of the nature of product "p", whether p corresponds to the goal pursued by A and is compatible with it is crucial in the determination of the outcome in the power complex.

It should be noted that the difference between the catatonic relationship and the commensal (and those following) is that in the former no distinction was made between i and i_c. The rationale is that if B is catatonic, it perceives only A's action directed to it and therefore, for A, i is equal to i_c. Further, it may be proposed that if a distinction is made between A's action i and its cost i_c toward the A/B power relationship, then B's action i' should also be distinguished from its cost. The proposition would make the distinction between *action* and *cost* obsolete if it were applied to both sides. The distinction in the case of A and not in the case of B is justified, because in our conceptualization Bi' is only that action of B

which is directly and totally involved in the power complex, while Ai may also be involved in other situations. Actions of B not related to the particular A/B power relationship are not counted in the equation in order to reflect a clear power situation. Of course, power situations are multi-directional, and we will need to repeat our computations for each direction and combine them for a more complete picture. Formally, we may then combine the different variables into:

$$(i' + A/i_c + pA) > (i_c + B/i' + pB) \longrightarrow P(A/B)$$

This formula is not an all-encompassing quantification for power, but is an attempt at encapsulating the variables conducive to a power relationship.[30] It also applies to our discussion of power relationships that follows. While by attributing comparable units to their components we may use our formula to measure specific and confined power relationships, the intangible dimensions of power impede its general quantification. Our further discussions will show, for example, that under certain circumstances the interactions, transactions and reactions of the components of a power complex may follow more the laws of direct and inverse proportionality than simple operations of addition, subtraction, multiplication and division.

SYMBIOTIC POWER RELATIONSHIP

Symbiosis here means interdependence and specialized coaction, involving some degree of mutuality between organisms of different kinds.[31] Defining symbiosis, Clements points out the large

---

30. On more sustained attempts at formalization see, *e.g.*, Goldman, 1972 and Nagel, 1975, and the latter for reference to other works.

31. Clements, 1935, p. 31.

III. Types of Power Relationships

and wide use of the term and adds that the mutuality of the coaction can fluctuate greatly from type to type. In our terminology "different kinds" do not necessarily imply totally unlike species. Two countries with different resources, or two parties with different ideologies, may become involved in a symbiotic relationship. In our model for power, a symbiotic relationship is different from a commensal one in that it is not a simple association.

Figure 3

In a symbiotic relationship as distinct from commensal, each of the components A and B of the power complex can move toward its goal only with the participation of the other. The difference can be demonstrated if we take our last example of landowner and farmer and turn it into a feudal-vassal relationship where the feudal prince is not much of a farmer and the vassal cannot have access to farmland without taking an oath of allegiance to the feudal prince for the land and his protection.

To illustrate further, we may say that a commander without an army or an army without a commander makes little sense. Another example is the negotiations between the oil-producing countries and oil companies.[32] The industrial societies of Western

Europe and Japan cannot function without the oil flowing from the countries of the Near and Middle East. Inversely, the oil-producing countries need the oil revenues which subsidize their budgets and finance their economic development and military ambitions.

The symbiotic model best illustrates the potentio-kinetic continuum and can be said to be most recurrent in power complexes, because the components of a power complex will usually combine, although the result will not be equally beneficial to the components involved. The bacterium may kill the legume in the long run.

DIVERGENT POWER RELATIONSHIP

Here we are presented with a model where the goals of A and B do not coincide. Or let us say, the model is for that part of A's and B's goals which do not coincide, because divergent power relationships may coexist with other models. By divergence we imply that the interests of A and B under consideration are not on a collision course -- we are leaving that for our next model.

Suppose B is a butterfly collector who has travelled to the American Midwest to pursue his hobby; but, influenced by A who is a geologist, B helps him prospect for mineral deposits. B is obviously not doing what he originally wanted to do. A may even-

---
32. The example fits our model, and also studies made of n-person games which end up in coalitions (notably Kalisch, et al., 1954). It will be interesting to compare the influence of the seating arrangements in the Kalish experiment with coalitions among oil-producing countries of different geopolitical areas. (See also Harsanyi, 1962b).

tually establish a mineral chart of the area. B may also succeed in interesting A in butterflies and make him spend some time running after them.

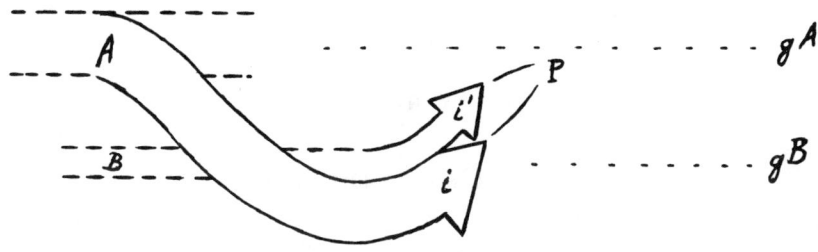

Figure 4

The more the vector of product p approaches gA, the more we can say that A has power over B and the more p will accrue to A.

CONFLICTING POWER RELATIONSHIP

This is what in game theory language corresponds to a zero-sum game. It is the extreme of opposing interests. What A wins, B loses, and is not willing to lose.

The likelihood that B will resist the exertion of power by A will be great and Ai_c may consist mainly of threat directed at B. There will also be a considerable amount of $\overline{Bi'}$, or a tendency to non-compliance on the part of B, which will have to be taken into consideration in the evaluation of Bi'.

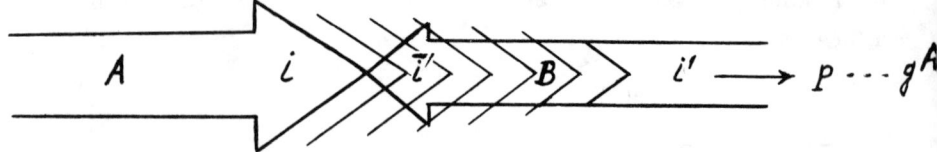

Figure 5

There are, of course, variations to the conflicting situations. *A* and *B* may be after the same indivisible goal and their clash may be competitive like that of two football teams. Or *A* may have designs to dispossess *B* of some of its sources of power, like two countries at war over a territorial dispute.

Our earlier models can turn into or involve conflicting dimensions. This may be the case, for example in the commensal situation of landowner *A* and farmer *B*, or their parallel version of feudal-vassal in the divergent model. If *A* goes for total submission of *B* in order to expand his land, or if *B* exploits *A*'s land for quick profit with a view to wresting it out of *A*'s hands, resulting in the erosion of the land, *A* and *B* will clash in their conflicting interests. For the symbiotic model the extreme of the predator and the prey relationship turns, of course, into an obvious conflict of interests.[33]

---
33.   Although, in a more general sense, the predator/prey relationship may still involve symbiosis. Take, for example, the fact that the carnivorous species, by its predation, regulates the growth of the food-species population which would otherwise have increased and gone extinct because of contagion or exhaustion of its own food supply. (Hawley, 1950 and Emerson, 1946, p. 13).

III. Types of Power Relationships

In the conflicting situation - more than in other models - the probability will exist that after a power confrontation there will remain a contestant to the product. The product accruing to A may have been a former possession of B. Of course, the outcome of the conflict may have been the total annihilation of one of the contestants, or, total absorption of one by the other: The product may have been B itself; an outcome which calls for a better understanding of the product.

IV

THE NATURE OF THE PRODUCT
OF POWER RELATIONSHIPS

Figuratively speaking, the chunk that A bites off B should be digestible. The presentation pA indicated the feedback of the power relationship's product into A's circuit. In absolute terms, not only should it be more substantial than the cost A has incurred ($pA > i_c$), but it should be compatible with A's resources and other power potentials. It should become part of A.

PRODUCT-COST REPLENISHMENT FUNCTIONS

The problem that arises is that of the product-cost replenishment relationship. The product may indeed be more important than the cost incurred, but it may be alien to A's organism or require a slow digestive process. Were the acquisition of the Grand Duchy of Warsaw by Russia at the Vienna Congress, or the occupation of Yugoslavia by Germany in World War II, desirable products of a power relationship? It was Bismarck's awareness of this problem which made him adopt a diplomacy of peace in Europe after the Franco-Prussian War in order to let time work for the cohesive assimilation of the components in the newly born German Empire.[34]

---
34. In conceptual analysis A is represented as a power continuum in time and space. Speaking in strict quantitative terms we can break down our

There may also exist a catch in the ratio between the cost and the product. True, the power relationship can be considered positive and rewarding for A when $pA > i_c$. But by how much? A power which uses a great quantity of its cognate resources to acquire a substantial quantity of an alien material may find its cohesion and composition weakened. To keep in line with previous examples, recall the case of the heterogeneous Austro-Hungarian Empire and its fate.

Thus in our potentio-kinetic evaluation of power we have to take into account: (a) the compatibility of the nature of the product of a power relationship with the nature of the powers it will be absorbed by,[35] and (b), depending on the consequences of (a), the ratio between the cost and the product. The measurement of this ratio is subject to the nature of the product for the obvious reason that the more the product is compatible with the nature of the receiving power the easier it can replenish the cost. These two dimensions imply (c) which would represent the rate of absorption of p into the potentials of the receiving power and its rate of convertibility into kinetic power. This last point also covers the more general question

---

analysis and conceive of A at time t' as A' when pA is being accrued to A. Then at t'' we can consider the process of absorption of pA into A as a new power complex A'' where the inner fermentations of A'' can be viewed as a new power complex of $(A-i_c)+pA$, which could be represented by other notations and the process of quantification renewed. We can, of course, conceive of A as the existential power at each of the t, t', t''... This is what we have done -- in computer language: LET A BE $(A-i_c)+pA$.

35. This implies that while A may receive a bigger portion of the product p, in the long run, B may come out of the deal stronger; because the portion of p it gets is cognate with its nature, while the part accrued to A is incognate to the latter.

IV. The Nature of the Product of Power Relationships

of convertibility of the potential resources as a whole into kinetic energy: How readily liquid and ready to be activated are a power's potentials?[36]

POTENTIO-KINETIC CONVERTIBILITY

Beside the product accruing to a power as a result of its transactions, its own cognate resources each have different degrees of convertibility. A country may have vast iron and coal resources, but may not have industrial and manpower capacities to turn those resources into machinery and weapons. What we are considering is the relationship between A as the total power potential and Ai as its kinetic action. Let us go back to Max Planck's stone on the wall. Standing atop the building, A can threaten B underneath that he will throw on him the massive stone if he does not comply with A's command. The stone, according to the laws of gravity, has indeed the potential of falling. But, if it were solidly and heavily cemented to the building, while we may calculate its potential according to physical laws by multiplying its weight and its distance from the ground, it does not constitute a power potential for A because he can not turn it into kinetic power; and B, aware of this fact, will not be impressed by his threat.[37] Now, suppose the stone in question is not solidly cemented, that A has a lever at his disposal which could topple the stone, and that B's possible movements underneath are limited. The potential fall of the stone is a threat to B if he does not comply with A's command.

---

36. Gamson, 1968, p. 94.

37. On non-fungibility of means of power, see Baldwin, 1979.

In this situation A's superiority over B is his position and the means which he can turn at will from potential into kinetic. A is powerful because he can make B feel his threat, making the latter comply with his demands without having to topple the stone. As long as this situation prevails, A keeps his power over B. What if A did topple the stone?

The moment the stone starts its free fall may seem the zenith of exertion of power by A over B. But it is also the moment when A ceases to have control over the means of its power. If the stone does not hit B, the power of A over B will be exhausted. If the stone does hit and crush B, with the elimination of B the power situation will altogether cease to exist (assuming, of course, that A was limited by the elements under consideration). The situation evokes Mao Zedong's famous thought to the effect that *"political power grows out of the barrel of a gun"*[38] which, in the light of our illustration, should be qualified by de Madariaga's lines: *"The gun that does not shoot is more eloquent than the gun that has to shoot and above all than the gun which has shot"*.[39] If A had a way of replacing the stone or lifting it back before it hit B, we would then need to re-evaluate the different situations.

Now suppose that next to B are C, D, E,...in situations similar to B, having limited possibilities of movement and threatened by toppling stones from A's position (and A has more stones -- President Reagan invaded Grenada and bombed Libya and had more ships, planes and missiles). While the isolated power relationship

---

38.   Mao, 1938 - 1966, p. 61.

39.   de Madariaga, 1929, p.57.

IV. The Nature of the Product of Power Relationships

between A and B will have ceased on the crushing of B by A's stone, the event may now be added to A's power potential in relation to C, D, $E \ldots n$ who, having witnessed the course of events, will be more clear about A's intentions. In this hypothesis A may have lost one power relationship but may have enhanced his reputation in relation to others.

Although our examples may have helped illustrate the kinetic concept of power, the addition of just one more dimension will show the complexity of power relationships and the difficulty to establish quantitative and mechanical patterns for them. Take, for example, a case in which the sight of B being crushed aroused A's religious and moral convictions and he renounced using his possibilities further. Not only will he no longer be in a power situation, but those under his control may ascend to his position and take over; that is, as soon as A's new dispositions have shown exterior signs. The injection of religious and moral convictions into the equations of power, however, moves us towards restraints and constraints imposed on power by a value system which, as we shall discuss in chapter IX, if shared by those submitting to power, could serve for the legitimization of power into authority.

V

SOURCES OF POWER

Our discussion of the convertibility of potential power into kinetic has led us into yet another dimension of our topic.[40] We

---
40. The classification in this chapter is not exhaustive. It is not intended as an attributional indexing either, but as an analytical tool for the understanding of relational dynamics. Our approach cuts across presentations by other authors which will be examined here under the headings of *sources* and *spheres* of power. The present part on *sources* will, in some ways, be an expansion on Dahl's division of "influence" (which we shall define later) into resources, skills and incentives (Dahl, 1967, p. 372, *et seq.*) and the non-normative parts of studies by Bachrach and Baratz, Nagel, Lukes, and Isaac. As pointed out earlier, we are making a distinction between power and the normative, legal and authoritative systems. At the same time we will include in this section some and in the section on *spheres of power* other hues of a spectrum which recent analyses of power have broadly established as follows:

Means--Domain--Scope--Extension--Reliability--Strength--Cost
(Bases) (Range) (Amount)

See notably Lasswell and Kaplan, 1950; Dahl, 1957, 1970; Bachrach & Baratz, 1962, 1963; Harsanyi, 1962; Nagel, 1968, 1975; Oppenheim 1982. Incidentally, the reader will notice that what was attempted so far was a feed-back process to link the two sides of this spectrum.

Means--Domain--Scope--Extension--Reliability--Strength--Cost
(Bases) (Range) (Amount)

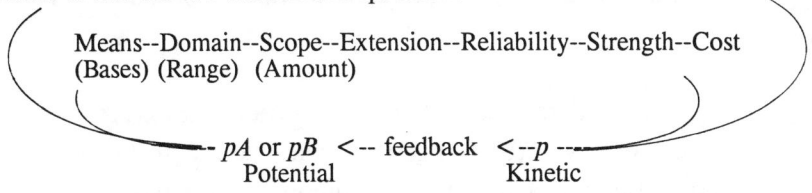

pA or pB <-- feedback <--p--
Potential   Kinetic

For other classifications of the sources of power see also Hobbes, *Leviathan*, Ch. X and MacIver, 1947, p. 87 *et. seq.*

are no longer talking about bricks and guns as sources of power, nor cement as a handicap to the use of power. We say that by throwing the first stone *A* could create a new dimension for his power - his stone throwing *reputation* with *C, D, E,* ...*n*. But his crushing of *B* could also create religious remorse in him, in many ways a bigger handicap than the cement of the wall. Of course, the action could also have had an inverse effect and removed his inhibitions about killing. The control to which we referred earlier, which the child exercises through his charm to get the candy, is obviously not based on physical force but is already a more complex phenomenon containing the ingredients of power. These are dimensions of power which need closer examination.

BRUTE FORCE

Brute force can, of course, give its holder the possibility of control. It lasts as long as it is forcefully superior. But its very simplicity and directness makes it vulnerable and breakable. Naked force can be easily evaluated and analyzed. It is like a piece of stone; it holds only by its weight and rigidity; when it hits other rigid phenomena weaker than itself, it breaks them; when it encounters superior force, it breaks. It can only be a part of the more complex and flexible phenomenon of power and should not be confused with it.

We need to add here a note on terminology.[41] In our dissection of power we are giving strict connotations to terms which in a broader sense can each be used as synonyms of power. Further-

---
41.　　　Keeping in mind footnote 8.

V. Sources of Power

more, it should be kept in mind that terms carry with them cultural, linguistic and ideological biases. In linguistic terms, some languages provide more or less flexibility for dealing with the concept of power. For example, the French language distinguishes between *puissance* and *pouvoir*. The first closer to force and strength but not quite synonymous with them -- as the French language has also the term *force*. *Puissance* is a more palpable concept of power.[42] It is used, for example, to identify foreign powers: *les puissances étrangères* -- those powers whose presence is felt at the border. The term is also used for energy such as electric power. *Pouvoir* has a more complex connotation and is more easily convoluted with authority.[43] *Pouvoir*, derived from the Latin word *poder* is both a noun and a verb. It is a doing power. In German, *Macht*, which stands for power, has a dynamic significance and is related to action through the verb *machen*. In English, *Macht* turned into might and *poder* and *pouvoir* turned into power. Both without a verb. Power is not something you can do; it is something to have and to be.[44]

---

42. Although the nuances of *pouvoir* and *puissance* must be recent linguistic developments as Montesquieu, for example, uses the two terms invariably and generally with reference to authority. Montesquieu, 1748, notably ch. XI. See also Aron, 1964.

43. This convolution has to do, to a large degree, with the French political culture. The Anglo-Saxon cultures of Great Britain and America, after decapitating their monarchs (literally in Great Britain and figuratively in the United States) passed power to the operators of liberal economy and made authority the business of a middle class democracy. The French, after decapitating their king ended up with a few more authoritarian kings and emperors and their power/authority conversion process developed into an elitist system where *l'autorité* kept its aura of authoritarian power and *le pouvoir* rang not without authority.

44. It would be of interest to study the semantics of comparable terms in other languages in their cultural and ideological contexts.

In our comparison of power and brute force, we could say that power has the potentialities of adaptation, resistance and pressure. In its encounter with a superior but simpler force it does not break, it can contract or retreat and withhold its potentialities without being irremediably crushed or broken. When in a favorable position, it can put on the rigidity of steel and give its adversary the fatal blow. It is the phenomenon which has retracted, yet has kept its potentialities and can make its pressure felt. The phenomenon that has been squeezed and takes its new squeezed shape without potentialities of pressure is not, in our analogy of power, a rubber ball or a spring. It is a piece of dough! Power is by its potentio-kinetic presence. Churchill, speaking of the movements of the German battleship Tirpitz towards the P.O. 17 convoy to Soviet Union in the Arctic in W.W.II, noted: *"The potential threat which they created had caused the scattering of the convoy. Thus their mere presence in these waters had directly contributed to a remarkable success for them."*[45]

In human terms, within the spectrum of brute force we can identify physical force (muscular) at one extreme, and certain aspects of stubbornness, fanaticism and determination -- individual or collective -- at the other extreme. These latter intangible factors are included within the concept of brute force because when certain character traits such as stubbornness or fanaticism reach the point of rigidified behavioral patterns they become comparable to brute force. The propulsion they produce is forceful and yet, in its rigidity and directness, vulnerable and breakable.

---

45.   Churchill, Vol. IV, p. 265.

V. Sources of Power

Take, for example, the character traits of Ayatollah Khomeyni of Iran in the 1980's. In the Iran-Iraq war of 1980-1988, with dogged stubbornness he mobilized his fanatical troops to withstand the shock of Iraqi attack. Yet, when there came the opportunity in July 1987 -- when Iran had the upper hand and Saddam Hussein had accepted the United Nations cease-fire resolution -- Khomeyni was not flexible enough to take advantage of it. While the situation involved more complex power components which we shall develop later, the case in point here is that Khomeyni's vengeful stubbornness was a factor in the continuation of the fighting to the detriment of Iran.

Of course, as it is for other sources of power, the evaluation of brute force is subjective and its outcome relative. Within the power complex, the assumption is that if B submits to A's forcible command it is because B finds submitting to A more agreeable than the consequences of A's coercive punishment. The assumption is subject to B's perception of pain and pleasure and his relationship with A. A masochist perceives pain differently from a paranoid.

MEANS

The means at a power's disposal are obviously of great importance. By means we refer to a spectrum extending from primary tools and weapons, which are nearer to the force end of the spectrum such as a stick, to more subtle means such as money and wealth. We are using the term "means" in its stricter sense -- close to its material and instrumental characteristics.[46] The term "means"

---
46. And in a different context than do the authors mentioned in our footnote 40.

can, of course, be given a broad connotation, particularly in the combination of means and ends, as done, for example, by Hobbes, mentioned earlier.[47] In that context, some have even gone so far as to emphasize the preponderance of means over the ends. In the words of Gandhi: *"They say 'means are after all means'. I would say 'means are after all everything'. As the means so the end. There is no wall of separation between means and end. Indeed the Creator has given us control (and that, too, very limited) over means, none over the end. Realization of the goal is in exact proportion to that of the means. This is a proposition that admits of no exception"*.[48] It is, of course, a question of semantics and what we want the term to cover. Gandhi is using the term "means" in a much broader sense than our meaning. As we noted in our discussion of force in the last section, terms can be given different connotations. In the broader sense, means can be used as a synonym for power; in particular when coupled with ends. What Gandhi says is that one needs power to achieve one's goals.

When used in that broader sense, the coupling of means and ends raises significant philosophical debate in different cultural and ideological contexts. The question becomes that of the justification of power's arbitrariness on its course to attain a given goal. Such are, for example, the exercises of power by revolutionary regimes. That the doings of power have to be justified implies the presence of a value system to which the power claims or wishes to adhere. Thus, the dictatorship of the proletariat, whose goal is the emancipation of the workers and the establishment of human rights,

---

47. *op. cit.* page 5

48. Bose, 1948, p.37. See our later discussion of the relativity of goals.

V. Sources of Power

may exploit the workers and oppress the people on its way to achieve the ultimate goal. Of course, a power which does not submit to a value system and does not aspire to justification and legitimized recognition is free from the means/ends constraints.[49]

Our narrower usage of the term "means" here -- limiting its connotation to instrumental and material sources of power -- permits us to dissect the components of power more closely and better analyze their areas of overlap.

POSITION

The position from which power is exercised is another crucial factor. The illustration given earlier of *A* atop the wall is at the primitive end of the spectrum. Let us use that example here to make a first assessment of the three different components singled out so far. *A* was in a favorable position atop the wall, his means were the stone and the lever, and he should have had the force to move them. As in the case of force and means, position can cover a spectrum going from the simple instance of a strategically favorable location to complex social situations.[50] The president of a bank, the governor of a state, the justice of the peace, each holds a position conducive to power. However, the aspect of the position we are considering here is not totally identical with what in those titles coincides with authority. What we are presently considering is neither

---

49.   See chapter IX.

50.   Michael Korda lists a whole array of power "positions", from the power spot in a cocktail party to the location of an office and the arrangements within it (Korda, 1975).

an office, nor exactly the right to the power that it legitimizes.[51] It is the power potential that a position can provide beyond the framework of its formal authority. Chamberlin, Churchill, Macmillan, and Thatcher were all British Prime Ministers. Of course, they exercised their authority under different circumstances and conjunctures. But it would be unreasonable to deny that, abstraction made of the circumstances and conjunctures, the kind and quality of the power each wielded was different.

A bank president has the authority to sign the grant of loans. But he does that mostly on the advice of his experts. In performing that function he may not be doing more than a post office clerk who has the authority to notarize signatures. Beyond that simple signature, however, the bank president holds a position which can radiate power. That depends very much on the person and the use he makes of the other sources at his disposal to wield power by exploiting his position. The bank president who exercises his duties strictly for the management of the bank and does not have a power base -- inside and outside the bank -- which inclines him to favor one direction as distinct from another, is not using his position for those particular power ends. Indeed, if he does not, he may not last long in his position unless he is there to buffer contending powers.

CONNECTION

This dynamic concept of position leads us to further sources of power. A power may tap its connections with other powers - not only vertically, but also laterally and diagonally to

---

51.   MacIver 1947, p. 83; Lasswell and Kaplan, 1950, p. 133.

V. Sources of Power

strengthen its own resources. Power A may call on power C for help in the A/B power relationship and return help to C in another context. The lateral connection between powers in the fluid area between their complexes implies that they perceive mutual benefit and compatibility and convergence in their interests as compared to other combinations: $(\exists AC)(AC \supset \sim AB \backslash\!/ BC)$. The imperative of connection leads powers to networking. In our earlier classification of power relationships we did not include a convergent power relationship. Because convergence, to the extent that it is lateral connection, while creating a "relationship", does not necessarily create a "power relationship". As the fluid area between power complexes that have lateral connections is filled by their respective expansions, the lateral connections may evolve into diagonal relationships which could be symbiotic or commensal and eventually turn into a hierarchy. In that sense connection and contact are, as we shall see later, *sine qua non* components of power which, besides being relational, is also hierarchical.

According to Parsons, "*While the structure of economic power is... lineally quantitative, simply a matter of more and less, that of political power is hierarchical; that is, of higher and lower levels. The greater power is power over the lesser, not merely more power than the lesser.*"[52] Of course, this qualification implies comparability. Without relationship and connection, it is not realistic to compare the power of a Soviet farm cooperative manager in Siberia with those of the Sheikh of Ras el Kheyma, a banker in London or a Medellín drug baron. Even where indirect relations exist but direct connections have not been established, one relational situation may not imply another. For instance, it does not necessarily follow that

---
52. Parsons, p. 126.

because *A* is more powerful than *B*, and *B* is more powerful than *C*, *A* is more powerful that *C*. The nature of the relationships may not be comparable, and as long as they are not connected in a power relationship -- whether by the intermediary of *B* or otherwise -- we cannot say that *A* has power over *C*. The *A/B* relationship may, for example, be professional, while the *B/C* relationship may be paternal or conjugal.

The assumption, however, is that where power relations exist, hierarchical imperatives arise. Even the lateral mutual help connection will not always remain on a par and will be subject to the interplay of the whole potentials of the components.

POWER OF PERSUASION AND INFLUENCE

Carrying on with connection, to secure *C*'s cooperation, *A* may need to persuade *C* that the product of their mutual assistance will benefit both of them. If *A* has a good power of persuasion he may draw a picture showing all the advantages to *C*, although, in fact, in the long run the outcome may be more profitable to *A*. This eventuality brings us to the power of persuasion as yet another source of power. Persuading *B* to do *i'* in a vertical power relationship is also one of the possibilities for *A* instead of using his force or material means. Depending on its magnitude, sphere and duration, persuasion could serve as one of the factors for the legitimization of power into authority, which we shall discuss later.

To persuade implies the capacity to influence or to have influence. Of course, the simple fact of having influence may not involve a power relationship. To illustrate our point, suppose you

V. Sources of Power

told your friend in a restaurant that a certain stock was likely to rise on the market, and someone next to your table overheard your conversation and as a result bought that stock -- something he would not have done otherwise. You have influenced him but you have not consciously exerted power upon him. Like other ingredients of power, only that part of influence which connects effectively will be part of a power complex.

Note our specification of influence as one of the ingredients of power and distinct from it.[53] The gradation from "having an influence on"[54] to "having control over"[55] can be established in the potentio-kinetic sense. The effect of A's action on B may be the creation of a disposition, or rather predisposition, for a changed behavior in the future.[56] B may not have complied the first time, but if he did the next time it may be because the leftover of A's last influence magnified the influence exerted upon him this time. That is, B would not have complied with A's desire or command this time if the last event had not taken place.

We may equally conceive of situations where the earlier influence may have an adverse effect on attempts at later control. Take for instance the guilt complex inculcated by the parents into a child against stealing and that child's inhibition to do so when asked by his parents in a desperate survival situation. We can extend that

---

53. See also Bell, 1975; Knorr, 1975; Barry, 1976; and, for a different tack on the distinction between influence and power, Morriss 1987.

54. Cartwright, 1969, p. 195.

55. Dahl, 1957, p. 207.

56. See notably Thibaut and Kelly, 1959, p. 101.

analogy to the consequences of unfair treatment of an adversary's population in a conflict by a nation upholding humanitarian principles -- the case in point is the public and media outcry in the United States against the use of "Agent Orange" in Vietnam.

The potentio-kinetic concept implies, of course, that the earlier influence and later control should be part of a continuum within a given power complex. If gang-leader A's threats do not induce member B to obey but create enough predisposition in him to obey later as a soldier faced with a superior threat from sergeant C, B's obedience to C should not be counted as the power of A over B.

B's inner disposition, however, is a factor that should be taken into account. We are thus recognizing the inner and outer properties of certain sources of power. It is in the fermentations and dynamics of the power complex that the internal properties of its components become effective. The external manifestations, however, become part of the power complex insofar as they correspond to an inner reality. That reality may or may not correspond to the external manifestations, *i.e.*, looking tough and in reality being tough or, as we shall see later, being aware of its own exterior manifestations by the entity emitting it.

SELF-CONFIDENCE, CHARISMA AND REPUTATION

The influence exerted on the eavesdropper in our earlier example in the restaurant may have been due to a confident tone. In other words, the apparent self-confidence of the person making the statement. Here we are speaking of the external appearance of self-

V. Sources of Power

confidence which may involve no power control. In a power continuum, as mentioned above, it should be coupled with consciousness.

In the long run, apparent self-confidence can remain a component of power if it reflects inner self-confidence and to the extent the person emitting it is conscious of it. This latter prerequisite has a reality of its own independent of the former; *i.e.*, a person who has little inner self-confidence may be conscious of the fact that because of some elements of his exterior appearance and personality, such as charisma, he radiates self-confidence, or he may discover that certain behaviors or attitudes indicate self-confidence and may adopt them. These are, of course, components of consciousness which we shall deal with shortly. Here, however, the point should be made that "acting" self-confident develops into a tool for attaining other components of power: For example, in certain contexts -- such as is often the case in the United States -- one of the crucial criteria in the selection of decision-makers is the demonstration of the capacity to make quick decisions. When a decision is called for, the clever aspirant to power takes the initiative of taking the decision -- whether he has sufficient reasons for doing it or not -- and distinguishes himself as a leader and a quick decision-maker. Keeping ahead of his mistakes -- where he has erred -- he may thus advance on the social ladder and acquire other sources of power.

Apparent self-confidence can thus be counted as a source of power. Its impact becomes evident when it is combined with other ingredients: force, means and position used with self-confidence; and self-confidence as a dimension of influence and the persuasive process. Charisma, mentioned in that context, may be a characteristic in its own right. But it is seldom separable from the power of persuasion and self-confidence. It may, of course, happen that a charismatic person is not necessarily self-confident, or that he inspires rather than persuades.

Back in the restaurant, we may find that the eavesdropper is influenced by the speaker's reputation. He may be influenced even by the reputation of the restaurant! Suppose he is an amateur investor having lunch in a restaurant near Wall Street known for being the rendez-vous of financial experts. Taking his neighbor at the next table, who behaves like a habitué of the restaurant, for a stock exchange expert he may be impressed by what he overhears and act upon it.

Reputation can be produced by other components of power. Consider the possibilities of combining means (money and mass media) with persuasive techniques (contents of mass media programs based on social psychology) and through publicity and propaganda creating a given power image. Reputation, however, implies a time-space continuum. In just about all human cultures, and even among some animals,[57] pedigree can serve as a source of power. It is the reputation the holder has inherited that produces the image. Where the name is known, a Rothschild is assumed rich until proven otherwise.

But above all, reputation is the manifestation of the potentio-kinetic nature of power. It is a present dimension of power,

---

57.　　See, for example, Cheney and Seyfarth, 1990, on family hierarchies among the Vervet monkeys.

based on the experience of its past behavior, plus the potentials available to it for future action. The hords of Jenghiz Khan became invincible as their reputation preceded them.

CONSCIOUSNESS AND WILL

In the human context, all this, of course, implies *knowledge* and know-how which, beyond implying specialized skills, should include the *general capacity to analyze, to evaluate, and to draw appropriate conclusions for action - including timing, improvisation as well as organization and planning.*[58] It is this capacity that can establish the relative value of the components of power, even the intangible ones such as self-confidence and reputation. A power can combine and exploit its potentials to extents which may exceed the possibilities of any one of the components in isolation. Its potentials include its awareness of external manifestations of its properties not corresponding to its inner realities, and its capacity to use them, in other words, *bluff*. *Courage* and *risk-taking* are components of power. In its analysis of possibilities, a power should relate its power position to other power complexes in the context of total environment. When Churchill asked his chiefs of staff on British preparedness to face the Germans, they replied:

> "Our conclusion is that prima facie *Germany has most of the cards; but the real test is whether the morale of our fighting personnel and civil population will counterbalance the numeri-*

---

58. For a treatment of organization as source of power -- and authority -- see Galbraith 1983.

cal and material advantages which Germany enjoys. We believe it will."[59]

Later events proved them right.

The knowledge factor is so important that it has become the subject of simplification for those who are in search of power but are incapable of essentially absorbing it. Knowledge has thus been reduced to information. "Information is power," so the saying goes. But information is only a tool of power which enhances power insofar as a power knows how to use it. Francis Bacon, that old hand at using different variations of power, had said *nam et ipsa scientia potestas est.*[60] Information is a most important tool for power. But if the capacity to use it is not present, information will be a computer ticking in the desert.

Power does not imply that the powerful "possesses" all the sources of power. Knowledge means knowledge about the availability of the sources of power and the capacity of combining and using them. Where A wants B to do something that it would not have otherwise done, and where C has strong and agile muscles and D has a club, A can exert power over B if it persuades D to give the club to C and C to hold the club over B's head so that the latter complies with the wishes of A. A, for all that matters, may be a midget.

The analytical and evaluative capacities of a power then cover not only the consideration of its own relationship with another

---

59.   Churchill, 1949, Vol. II, p. 89.
60.   Francis Bacon, 1597, "On Heresies".

V. Sources of Power

power, but also the analysis and evaluation of the conflicting natures of other powers or simply different textures and shades of those powers in their relationships. Thus one power complex may use other powers against each other or combine some of them against some others in situations beneficial to itself. Great Britain remained a great power through the 18th and 19th centuries partly because she successfully played this balancing game in the European power complex.[61]

Parenthetically it should be emphasized that while cognition, consciousness, will, knowledge and the capacity to manipulate information have been enumerated as components of power, wisdom and sagacity have not been included as its *sine qua non* characteristics. While intelligence and cognitive elements of wisdom can be used for power ends, wisdom and sagacity in themselves may not aspire to power. Indeed, history is fraught with powerful wisdom midgets.

Our parenthetical remark leads us to two "factors" of social power, namely, *competition* and *ambition*. They are not sources of power but rather propulsing factors for the realization of power. They are social manifestations of the will to power and domination drive discussed earlier and account for the existence of powerful wisdom midgets. History is lamentably short of philosopher kings. What it is rich in are ambitious, shrewd operators manipulating the sources of power to get on top of the heap; modelling themselves after *The Prince* of Machiavelli rather than taking inspiration from the *Meditations* of Marcus Aurelius.

---

61.   See Morgenthau, 1967, p.189. In terms of game theory see, for example, the concept of *pivotal* power in Shapley and Shubik, 1954.

These factors translate into such social theories as the survival of the fittest, and the selfish interest motives of capitalism, and are social realities reflected in processes of legitimization of power into authority which we shall touch upon later. In the democratic process, for example, the operators may manage to get the money from the rich (notably through contributions to the candidate's party or campaign funds), support from a give-and-take network of other operators and potential cronies, and the votes from the multitude (by using the money of the rich to persuade the people through the media to vote for the candidate). They can project an image of wit and intelligence by employing speech-writers and devise their strategies and policies by picking the brains of the intellectuals. In different systems it is the manipulation of the apparatus by operators and apparatchiks. It produces representatives, senators and presidents. Of course, what interests us more here is their will to power and their consciousness about the ways to get it rather than the authority attributes of their position.[62]

The relationship between the will to power and the ways for its attainment is crucial for the understanding of the entelechy of power. The saying: "Where there is a will, there is a way" is true insofar as the two propositions are connected, *i.e.*, the person who wills power knows the way and engages in it. The case which best illustrates our point is probably that of Nietzsche, *the* philosopher of the "will to power".[63] Conscious and cognizant of his own will to

---

62.   See the distinction made earlier under "Position".

63.   Nietzsche, 1886, 36.

V. Sources of Power

power, Nietzsche, who longed for audience and disciples, did not know how, or disdained, to engage in the processes and compromises which would have make him powerful.[64] The will we are referring to as a crucial source of power is will-power rather than a will to power. It is neither a schopenhaueresque incessant impulse of the will to live, nor Nietzsche's entire instinctive life. While it addresses human cravings, will-power itself is not craving; it is determined and is capable to exert power. It is the characteristic which, conscious of the sources of power, turns them into power. In social terms, the potential power of Nietzsche's philosophy of the will to power devolved to his sister. Through organization and exploitation of other sources of power -- hers and her brother's position, connection, influence, reputation and knowledge -- Elisabeth Förster-Nietzsche actualized the potential power of Nietzsche's philosophy into the audiences and disciples Nietzsche had so longed for.[65]

In our review of the sources of power we have gradually moved from the more elemental to the more cognizant. As a simple illustration, one may say that the water behind a dam is only force. Before the dam was built, the downhill flow of water was brute force rolling boulders down the mountain; after the dam is built, it becomes tamed force with potentials to generate electric power. But no power will be produced if the valves of the dam are

---

64.   Walter Kaufmann, in his translation of *Ecce Homo*, draws our attention to a passage where Nietzsche, comparing Wagner to himself, declares his *"will to power as no man ever possessed it."* In "On the Birth of Tragedy", sec.4.

65.   As revealed in his literary work and correspondence, notably, Nietzsche, 1971, 1975. See our later discussion of the "Coefficients of Power" and the devolution of power. For variations on the concept of will see Descartes, 1644, I,32 *et seq.*; Spinoza, 1677(b), proposition XLVIII *et seq.*; Locke, 1689(a), notably ch. XXI; Kant, 1798; Schopenhauer, 1818; and Nietzsche.

not opened and the water is not permitted to become *active* by its movement. If there were no turbines and generators behind the valves, the movement of water would simply turn into forceful streams. It is in its *contact* with the turbines and generators -- which put up a relative resistance but rotate under the pressure of the forceful stream -- that the water becomes *effective* in generating power. The power-holders, however, are those who create the *incremental potential* by holding the water behind the dam and put it in contact with the generator and decide on the distribution of electricity. The power they control is the potential energy which the high level of water holds behind the dam. *Power can thus be conceptualized as the conscious incremental potential of an actor who is active, in contact and effective.*[66]

The *consciousness* of power may remain at the stage of knowledge, i.e., as a potential source of power. In our earlier example of marksman A, it would correspond to a situation where A is aware that his marksmanship has impressed B, but does not exploit it to establish a power relationship. In our potentio-kinetic conceptual framework, for A's consciousness to become a positive element of his kinetic power, the existing power relationship must have been brought about by A's *intention and will*.

Of course, A's will in its net form is aimed at gA originally set as A's goal. The product of the power relationship may not, as we saw earlier coincide with A's goal. The discrepancy between gA and p may be due to factors beyond A's control. The more A is conscious, in the potential sense, of the factors beyond its

---

66.   For a mechanical illustration of consciousness developing into its human dimension, see Deutsch, 1963, p. 98 *et seq.*

control which may affect his power relationship, the more he will adjust his will, in the kinetic sense, such that gA will be near to p. What is implicated here is the subjectivity of both consciousness and will and their relevance in the potentio-kinetic spectrum. The factors beyond A's control include the consciousness and will of those upon whom A wills to exercise power. Those consciousnesses and wills are in turn subjective variables with different degrees of flexibility. Beyond the circumstances and conjunctures which are not controllable by powers involved, the product of their power relationship will depend on the interplay of their capacities to analyze, evaluate and draw appropriate conclusions for action -- and their potentials to adapt to and absorb the consequences of one action in order to move on to subsequent actions.

VI

COEFFICIENTS OF POWER

Subjectivity of analysis and evaluation on the part of powers involved, discussed in the last chapter, may also bring about a product which may be more favorable than the goal fixed by a given power. Suppose, for example, that in B's consciousness, A's intentions of reprisal are exaggerated. Moved by what, according to Brentano, "is the subject's relationship to a content, or the direction of an object (which need not be the reality)" B accomplishes an act beyond A's expectations.[67] The discrepancy between A's intentions and B's "*Vorstellung*"[68] of them may be due to B's misperception -- or knowledge -- about a degree of A's capacities, of which A may not be conscious. While the product of the power relationship accrued to A may have been greater than the goal fixed by A because of the above discrepancy, the cause of the discrepancy itself, *i.e.*, A's additional "capacity", cannot be considered as A's power potential unless A becomes conscious of it and takes advantage of it. The discrepancy as a potential may go wasted until A or B or a third party C becomes conscious of it and uses it as a source power.

---

67.   Brentano, 1924, Vol. 1, p. 124.

68.   *Vorstellung* is the German word used by Brentano which means imagination, representation, conception or idea.

The case may best be demonstrated by its extension *ad absurdum* to the total non-existence of *A*. If *A* exists only in *B*'s frame of mind -- a proposition advanced by Nagel and picked up by Dahl[69] -- can we objectively say that *A* has power? In the imaginary world of *B* there exists the phenomenon *A* which we should take into account when we analyze *B*'s behavior. As *A* does not exist in reality, we should see where the spoils of *B*'s behavior in relation to the imaginary *A* end up. Nagel's example of the Japanese surrender because of the fear of more atomic bombs does not accrue to non-existent bombs but to the U.S. The beneficiaries of the *Vorstellung* of the totem, god, goddess or Santa Claus[70] are the temple priests and other social relationships.

Granted, this is a strict empirical approach. As much as the follower of the particular god or goddess may not be able to substantiate its existence, we will not necessarily be able to prove its non-existence. The fact, however, is that existing or not, the thing or non-thing has manifest power. Many authors have pointed out the magic dimension of power.[71] This non-existential dimension as a source of power entangles us with "power-in-itself". The subjective psychological dispositions do not seem to provide all the answers.

The voodoo death or physical disorder may be explained as a psychosomatic reaction of the subject to a taboo.[72] But the taboo

---

69. Nagel, 1968, p.132, footnote 10, and Dahl, 1970, p.31.

70. March, 1955, p.444.

71. Merriam, 1934; Russell, 1938; de Jouvenel, 1945; Lapierre, 1953-69; Ruyssen, 1957.

72. Cannon, 1942; Richter, 1957.

VI. Coefficients of Power

does not cease after its effect is produced. It is rather enhanced. The definitions given by Codrington of *mana* and quoted by Durkheim can bring some light to our discussion: *"There is a belief in a force altogether distinct from physical power, which acts in all ways for good and evil; and which it is of the greatest advantage to possess or control. This is Mana...... It is a power or influence, not physical and in a way supernatural; but it shows itself in physical force, or in any kind of power or excellence which a man possesses. This mana is not fixed in anything, and can be conveyed in almost anything"*.[73]

In existential sense, skeptical but cognizant of this subliminal and sublime "power-in-itself" at the empirically "non-existential" state (a contradiction in terms), we may have to conceive of a coefficient to the sources and resources of power. The assumption being that the whole may be more than the sum of its parts. Thus, simple additions and multiplications of different sources of power may not give us a whole picture of power. A parallel can be found in nuclear physics. The weight of an atom is less than the weight of the protons and neutrons comprising it. The weight discrepancy is compensated by a relatively enormous amount of energy within the atom.[74] Where are we to look for the coefficient

---

73. Durkheim, 1912, p. 194; see also Slater, 1966 and Fogelson and Adams, 1977, therein, notably, the article by Margaret Mackenzie.

74. For example, in the case of helium atom comprised of two protons, and two neutrons, the atomic weight of the two isolated protons (1.00812 x 2) and two isolated neutrons (1.00893 x 2) is 4.0341. The helium atom weighs 4.0039; there is a difference of 0.0302. This infinitesimal weight discrepancy is compensated by the energy held within the helium atom. The weight multiplied by the square of the velocity of light according to Einstein's theory ($E = mc^2$) represents seven million times the energy released by the combination of a carbon atom with an oxygen to produce a molecule of carbon dioxide in the familiar process of combustion. Craven, 1964, pp. 15-16.

of power? The Bergsonian *élan vital* did not apply only to groups, armies, societies and what we know as living beings. Bergson compared the power of human mind to the potential energy stored in an atom.

The coefficient of power in socio-political terms turns into what we may call the *"engrossment factor"* -- feedback which engrosses power. Engrossment does to human relations what a laser does to photons and a transistor does to electrons. Like photons and electrons it should be measurable. The problem is that it is lodged within humans; hard to measure. But just because it cannot be measured, we cannot discarded it. Discarding it would be like ceasing to observe, in order to understand, the universe, because we cannot count the stars. Engrossment factor was the charge and the goose bumps which the intonation of *Sieg Heil* in the Nuremberg rallies created in those who shouted it and the elation it produced in the Nazi party leaders on the podium who felt engrossed to go onto grosser deeds. Or, replace the elements in the equation with the mollahs and the masses shouting "Down with America" in the Iran of 1980's. Surely, there is acquiescence in the assembled masses in these examples which is the authority attribute of the power holders.[75] After all, the German people voted the Nazis into the Reichstag through free elections, and the mollahs are legitimized by the power of Allah. But there is also a charge which is different from that of a sedate assembly listening to a reasonable and calm politician. The charge goes beyond Le Bon's mental unity of the crowd and their collective mind.[76] It is a controlled and organized

---

75.   See our later distinction of power and authority in Chapter IX.

76.   Le Bon, 1903, p.27 *passim*; see also Canetti, 1962; Hofstätter 1957.

VI. Coefficients of Power

charge for the engrossment of power. The crowd, compared to a controlled and organized mass, is what a flashlight is to a laser. Hitler was quite conscious of those properties. To turn the photons of the flashlight into the deadly rays of a laser, to convert the individual *Vorstellung* potentials into the engrossment factor, to transform the energy of the masses into a coherent tool for power, Hitler observed:

> *The receptivity of the great masses is very limited, their intelligence is small, but their power of forgetting is enormous. In consequence of these facts, all effective propaganda must be limited to a very few points and must harp on these in slogans until the last member of the public understands what you want him to understand by your slogan.* "[77]

In interpersonal relations, the coefficient of power is the boss's feeling of omnipotence after denying promotion to a subordinate, not because of his lack of qualification, but because he was irreverent in his behavior towards the boss -- that is, to the extent the boss senses his power in doing so and does not feel remorse or doubt for his action. The coefficient of power is also what in the relationship of the boss with another subordinate, whom he has promoted, turns into respective feelings of magnanimity and loyalty.

Magnanimity and *loyalty* are terms conveying power and its dynamics. They are power attributes which transcend and, from within, corrode law and authority. The magnanimous leader, king or president, pardons the convict. A loyal servant does not

---

77. Hitler, 1943, 1971, pp.180-181. See also Lenin, 1902; Mao 1938.

denounce his master who may have committed an unlawful act. The subordinate covers up the boss's mischiefs. Loyalty has the primitive and anti-social in it. It has the elements of charisma, influence and persuasion on the one hand; and belonging, security, looking-uptoism and fear on the other hand. It is what holds the bands of pirates and the gangs of Los Angeles and New York together.

Decatur's "...*our country, right or wrong*" had some of it. While nationality is a legal concept based on the norms of international law, nationalism is imbued with loyalty. While nationality provides for rights and responsibilities, nationalism generates pride and sacrifice and serves as the coefficient of the power of a nation. It is what, beyond the need for security and greed, adventure and curiosity, made Western powers become great in the 19th and 20th centuries. It is the component which, together with industry and balance of payments made Japan a power in the latter part of the 20th century. Collectively, the coefficient is *esprit de corps*. The consciousness of power is not exactly that of the rational man. One could say that if one has never felt power, one would not be able to understand the proposition. But then, everybody has.

Merriam, approaching the concept of power as an element of balance and equilibrium for social situations, shows, in his chapter on the Family of Power, the omnipresence of power as the dimension of any group - whether a state or a band of pirates.[78] If we generalize the term "group" to encompass not only human or animal groups, but any group which has a cohesion, we may come close to the atomic illustration and conclude that the cohesion of the

---
78.   Merriam, 1934.

VI. Coefficients of Power

group, be it an atom, a tree, a group or a constellation implies the existence of power. Without it no group structure or movement can be conceived.

Viewed thus, power, being the prime mover, could be sought and maintained for its own sake. Many schools of thought, from the legalist philosophers of China to the political thinkers of modern Europe, have pleaded the case of power.[79] Power-in-itself, however, cannot exist in itself as an essence. It is power, as we saw earlier, in so far as it is in contact, active and effective. Even the "non-existent" taboo, mana or the totemic principle *is* to the extent of its effectiveness and impact over its subjects. Power is not loose and total freedom. That would equate to total absence of power. Power is not freedom; it *is* by the degree of its *freedom of action* over its sphere of power. A look at the spheres of power may help us examine further the existential conditions of power.

---
79.   Shang-Chun, 4th Century B.C.; Han Fei Tzu, 3rd Century B.C.; Machiavelli, (1513) 1532; Hobbes, 1651; Treitschke, 1863...; Nietzsche, 1883-1889; Gumplowicz, 1885.

VII

SPHERES OF POWER[80]

To be active, in contact and effective, power must mesh with the elements which it has or wants to have power over. In the process of entanglement to gain power, those who seek dominant positions may confine their freedom. Power has been generally likened to a pyramid because at every stage of the struggle for domination only some of those at the bottom will move up, and by the very nature of the situation dominate those who remain in the lower strata. The repetition of the process results in a pyramidal shape and by definition, a pyramid has a wide base and is narrow at the top.

Figure 6

---

80.   Parts of this section are reproduced from Khoshkish, 1979.

But the pyramid of power in not a static geometric form. Its dynamics and fermentations require permanent exercise and affirmation of the power which shapes it. Within it, there will be constant contacts, interactions, transactions, and counteractions among complexes which make it a whole. (Figure 6).

Power, if it is power, is ever evolving. It is for the sake of simplicity of presentation that at this stage we have pictured it as a plain pyramid. Like all other socio-political phenomena, power should not be visualized as a hard piece of concrete, but as a flux in which every particle is an interacting factor in the whole. Figuratively, in its dynamics and fermentations, a power complex, like a viscous crystal, should be able to go from extreme rigidity to the near weightlessness of a light gas. Within any relationship there is an optimum stage between rigidity and weightlessness where power, depending on its texture, can function best. At the rigid extreme it may exercise brute force -- an effective instrument under certain conditions -- while under other circumstances it may diffuse and lighten its pressure over its components or opponents so that its weight may scarcely be felt, and yet it may remain in control.

The top of the pyramid sits best, of course, when it distributes weight evenly over the base. In political terms, this happens when power exercises equal control and/or care over different components of its complex. Depending on its fluidity, it may have a greater or lesser freedom of action when it shifts its control and/or care within a tolerable radius.

VII. Spheres of Power

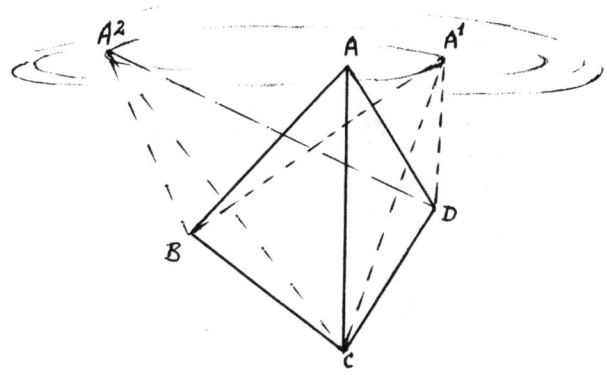

Figure 7

In position *A1* in Figure 7, the top of the pyramid is distanced from points *B* and *C* of the base and other points along the connecting lines *A1B* and *A1C* as compared to the *A1D* line. *A1* either controls the *A1D* area of the pyramid more or gives it more attention and/or care. Yet it seems still to be in balance, because in its overall situation, its relation to *D* compensates its distance from *B* and *C*. In position *A2* the power holder seems to be in a more precarious situation. It is off-balance and may fall. The shifting of control and emphasis by the summit of the pyramid is, of course, an involved process within the different strata of the complex.

The points of pressure and support may not be identical and uniform from top to bottom. Each point of control within the complex may have a greater or lesser radius of oscillation, depending on its viscosity. There are, within the complex, "proximate policy makers".[81] (Figure 8).

---
81.   Lindblom, 1970, p. 70 *et. seq.*

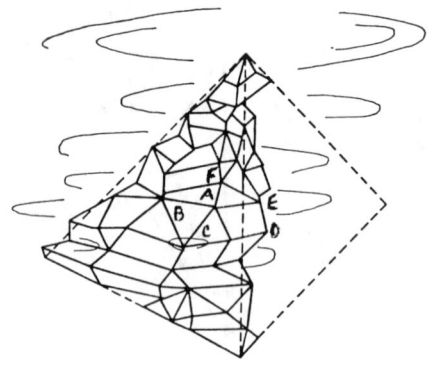

Figure 8

In a corporation, union, political party, or Mafia, we could focus on a sector such as *ABCDEF* in Figure 8 for closer scrutiny and examine its relationship with other sectors and the whole. We may find that in its immediate environment it has a better (or worse) reputation, or is (or is not) solidly controlled. Recognizing and conditioning the domination drives of different components of a power complex and accommodating within it the resistants -- which we will discuss in the next chapter -- are essential for the control and exercise of superior and encompassing power. Evaluation of degrees of control possible, their loci and their nature will be crucial for the efficiency of a power complex. The conqueror king, in order to rule a larger territory, may have to divide the conquered land among his lieutenants; the professional association, in order to accommodate a large number of members subdivides into specialized groups providing multiple turfs. The diffusion may dilute the encompassing power but may also serve as its means for better control. Providing the components that have their own spheres of identity with prerogatives of inclusion and exclusion

VII. Spheres of Power

will develop illusory or real power which they would want to guard against each other, creating the need for the encompassing power's arbitration. Divide and rule is a precept for power. Those who exercise or are delegated to exercise power at different levels and sectors of the pyramid thus share, drain or enhance the power of the summit and the whole.[82]

Power has the possibility not only to oscillate within a radius on a plane as in Figure 7, but also to compress or dilate, thus condensing or rarefying relationships among its components (see Figure 9).

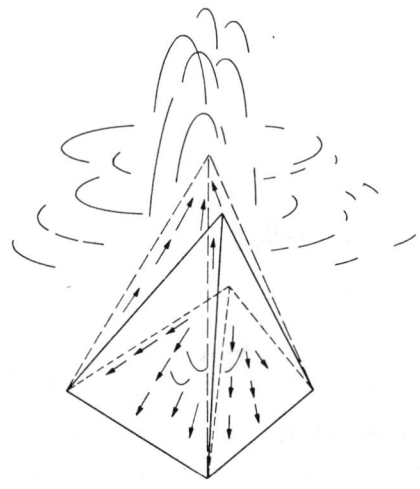

Figure 9

---
82.   In Lukes' terms, agents which exercise power within systems and structural determinants. See, notably, Lukes 1974, 1978 and 1979, keeping in mind the possibility of confusion between power and authority.

Power may compress when it needs better control of a situation or when the components require closer relationship in order to give better cohesion to the whole. The compression may take place also at the base and the power-holder may, or may have to, relinquish grounds in order to keep the same angle of power within remaining components; otherwise, a compression from the top, without reducing the expanse of the bottom, will flatten power-holder's controlling position. (Figure 10).

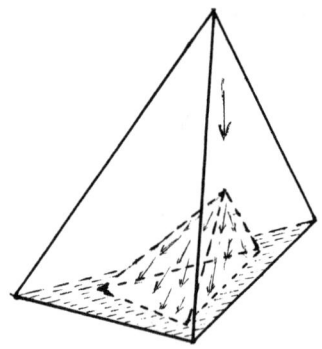

Figure 10

Flattening implies reduction of power components, such as a reverse process in a cumulative economy which, if continued to the extreme, could revert to a subsistence level where there would be few ingredients for building a substantial power pyramid.[83] The

---

83. For an elaboration on subsistence and cumulative economies see Khoshkish, 1979, pp.40-47.

model applies to a variety of instances such as the retreat and regrouping of an army, the retrenchment of a business, or reduction in the international commitments of a nation.

On the other hand, a power may initiate dilation when a condensation within the complex calls for easing of controls. It may also be a prelude to an elation of power strata preparing for further expansion. (Figure 11).

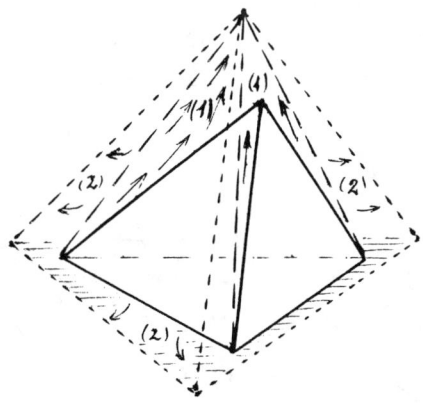

Figure 11

But an elation without possibilities for expansion at the base, distancing the upper strata of the power complex from the base, may reduce its stability. For example, in the complex French politics of the 1960's, de Gaulle envisioned a superpower foreign policy which many of his countrymen, more concerned with crucial domestic problems, did not share with him. His posture gave an impression of aloofness resulting in the dissatisfaction and alienation of some of his popular base and culminating in the 1968 events and the uprising of the students and workers' strikes.[84]

Shifts, compressions or dilations of power create different relationships and ratios within the power complex, upsetting the prevailing habits, frustrations and expectations, and perhaps eventually changing its nature and course. A party leadership which starts shifting to an emphasis on workers' rights will eventually embrace more of the ideologies of trade unionism and socialism than those of free enterprise. The shift may take place because of a prior trade unionist penetration into the leadership of the party. (Figure 12).

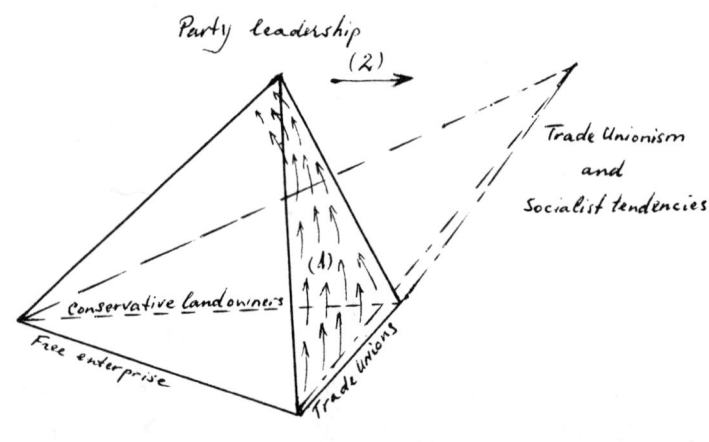

Figure 12

---

84.   In his own words: "Sur la pente que gravit la France, ma mission est toujours de la guider vers le haut, tandis que toutes les voix d'en bas l'appellent sans cesse à redescendre." de Gaulle, 1970, p. 314. Something had to give and did. But in the meantime de Gaulle managed to pull the country back on her feet; with some kicking and screaming.

VII. Spheres of Power

Or it may be caused by policy-makers who, although not of trade unionist origin themselves, may have detected favorable grounds among the workers. In the latter case, if the shift persists, the party's rank-and-file may gradually be penetrated by trade unionist elements. (Figure 13).

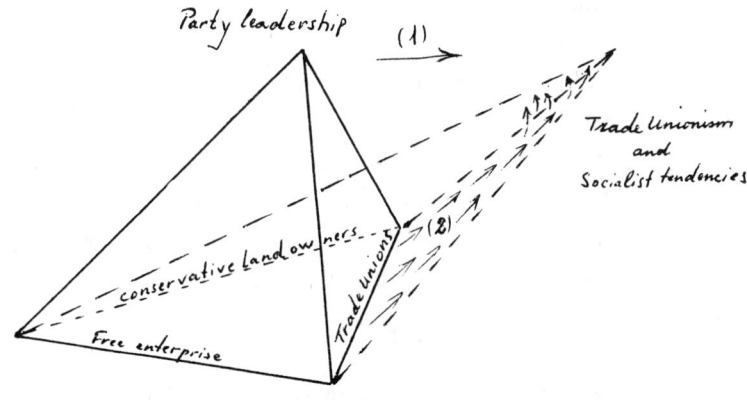

Figure 13

In general terms, growing emphasis on the role of certain sectors of the power complex may amount to the passage of some power potentials to those sectors -- a trend which may not be reversible and which may eventually change the power relationship patterns or even the nature of the power complex. A father who permits his son to use the family car, both to make the son more useful in doing family errands and to give his son more liberties, will have less control over the car than before. It will be difficult to revert to the earlier situation and prohibit the son's use of the family car without compensation or friction. Similarly, the industrialist who, after having run his enterprise on the basis of his individual will and decision-making, agrees to take into consideration the views of the workers, will have a hard time reverting to individual rule. But his recognition of workers' views, although changing the power relationship, may create more interest and incentive in the workers, improve the production, and in the long run, give the industrialist possibilities of expansion. It has, nevertheless, changed the power relationship within the pyramid.

In dilation of a power complex, the sum total of control is not always reduced but diffused and dispersed among the different strata and components of the power complex. The liberalization of the Catholic Church under John XXIII and Paul VI gave new vigor and credibility to the faith, but at the same time made open dissent among the clergy possible on such matters as birth control and political activism.

Khrushchev's recognition of the possibility of national roads to socialism in the 1950's loosened the lid which had been tightly placed by Stalin over Eastern Europe. It resulted in the uprising in Hungary and later liberalizations in other Eastern European countries. The Soviet Union had to use force both in Hungary and Czechoslovakia and stretch Brezhnev's "umbrella" over Eastern Europe to regain control. In this case the controlled elements in a situation of dilation moved towards disintegrating the very power structure itself.

In the process of liberalization, the relationship of the Soviet Union with the socialist countries of Eastern Europe changed. Even after the formulation of the Brezhnev doctrine the dilation created by that first phase of de-stalinization diffused some of the

VII. Spheres of Power

Soviet power in Eastern Europe. In exchange, despite its military interventions, Soviet Union gained some influence among the third world countries. It may have been argued that the Soviet Union would have gained even greater influence in other parts of the world had it not used naked force against deviations in Hungary and Czechoslovakia.

But timing and dosage of the use of power and its dilation or compression are complex. Had the Soviet Union not intervened in Hungary and Czechoslovakia, the dispersion and diffusion of power may have had consequences which would have changed beyond recognition the very nature of Soviet power. The changes could not have taken place solely in the relationships and ratio of control within that power complex without affecting factors beyond it which could have proven detrimental to its very existence.[85] The upheavals in Eastern Europe and the Soviet Union since Gorbachev's glasnost and perestroika underscore that argument.

Variations in the visual presentations of the pyramid could illustrate different political power complexes. The power structure of a less-developed and unevenly distributed economy with an autocratic regime could be presented with a wide base and a narrow peak, the mass of people constituting the lower strata. So could be the power structure of a police state with modern techniques of mass control: lethal coercive means, secret police information network and efficiently controlled mass media. (Figure 14).

---

85. These last three paragraphs are textual transcriptions from our study on power presented in 1971. See the Preface.

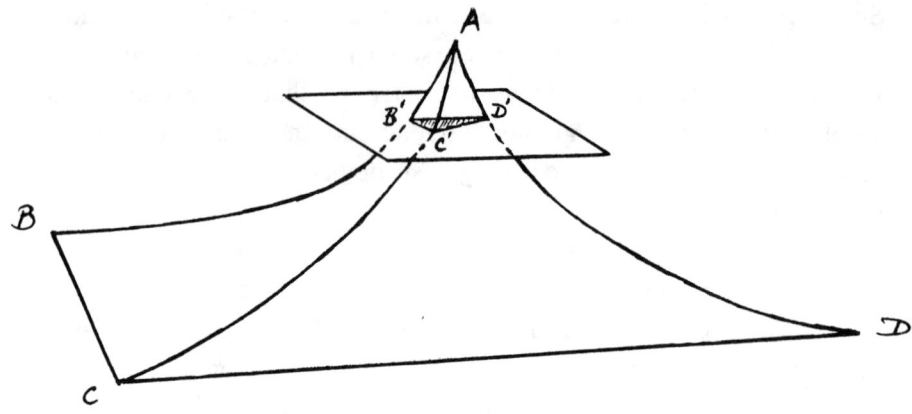

Figure 14

The power may seem to sit on solid and absolute bases. An analysis of the top of the pyramid may show, however, that the power-holder's position is not necessarily soundly established; that is, if it is not buttressed by factors of legitimization of power into authority. In examining political power in particular, as we shall touch upon later, authority is intertwined with the power properties of the complex and should not be confused with it. The ruling strata may, for example, exercise its power legitimized by the religious beliefs of those submitting to it. So, the pyramid of power of the Sultan of Brunei will be different from what was that of Noriega in Panama. In the complex represented in Figure 14, while the ruled at the lower level are suppressed or subservient and may not be able to challenge the power structure because of tight control or relative passivity of the base, the power struggle takes place within the upper strata in the form of court intrigues, junta bargains and coups (the surface of support for A where the plane cuts the pyramid at intersection $B'C'D'$). Such was, for example, the case of Duvalier in Haiti. The proposition is, of course, valid as long as the base is deprived

VII. Spheres of Power

and subservient. When the base, through factors such as economic development, better education or communications and/or external factors, becomes politically aware and active, the power structure will undergo change, civil strife, upheavals and revolution. Such were the cases of the rule of Muhammad Reza Shah in Iran, Batista in Cuba or Somosa in Nicaragua. The presentation covers many contemporary societies in Latin America and the Middle East. It is also applicable to many European post-Reformation kingdoms, and the Romanovs in Russia.

The power structure of more developed and distributive economies will have fewer non-participating members at the base and the controls within it depend more on diffusion of power subject to law and authority structures. (Figure 15).

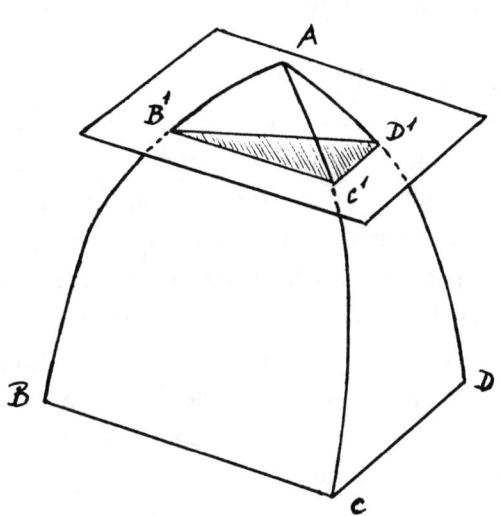

Figure 15

The rounder the edges of the pyramid, the more integrated and diluted, the more consensual, the more law and authority oriented and the less concentrated the power complex will be. Some social theories have conceived of rounding the edges of power to the point of turning it into a sphere. Such theories assume that in a perfect power distribution and participation the lack of a base and seat of power is compensated by the fact that power participation is so enlarged that no matter how the sphere rolls the structure will hold together. In such a complex, whatever is on top will assume the responsibilities of the top, and the bottom will play the role of the base: anarchy in the "utopian" sense of Owen and Fourier, and younger Marx's communism. The hypothesis is, of course, utopian. The communal experiments that have survived are those such as the Hutterite communities where power is intertwined with strong religious and communal controls establishing strict hierarchies.[86]

A more realistic pyramid for a developed and reasonably distributive economy is a bellied pyramid as illustrated in Figure 15, where the middle class is substantial and the diffusion of power is significant. Looking at the top of such a pyramid, we see that the power-holders are not pointing sharply upwards as in the autocratic regimes. The status differentiation is smaller at the top where the power structure is solidly situated (section *B'C'D'* in Figure 15). But then what it has is more authority, and less power, accountable to below. The President of the United States is not in great danger of being overthrown by a coup. But he mostly exercises legitimate power, i.e., authority, and shares power with the

---

86. See Khoshkish, 1976, and our later discussion of legitimization of Power into Authority.

VII. Spheres of Power

Congress and the Supreme Court and, in more general terms, is influenced by all the other political machinery of the country, including state governments, parties and pressure groups. This implies, of course, as the figurative presentation can suggest, a greater surface of support and consequently a greater surface of friction. In other words, in an economically more developed and politically more participatory complex with a diffusion of power, the power-holders have less chance of whimsical action. The pyramid also shows the weight of the middle class on the lower part of the pyramid and its magnitude as a whole. This corresponds to the formula of substantial middle class for stable political institutions advocated from Aristotle to our day.

Whatever the static illustration of the pyramid, the power complex, in its dynamics, more closely resembles the sphere; not the utopian sphere of law and harmony, but a more energetic and unsettled one where the power-holders seek the center rather than some peripheric heights. Combining the different dimensions of power dynamics as discussed in the last pages and superimposing Figures 7, 8, and 9, we find the power complex appear as a sphere not unlike illustrations of atomic structures. (Figure 16).

In that analogy, the identification of a power complex will depend on what kind of an atom it resembles. Some atoms hold together better just as some power complexes do. There are radioactive and actinide atoms with more or less short spans of life which decay and emit energy, and their interaction with their environment alters their nature.[87] There are atoms whose cohesion is such that

---

87. A uranium-239 nucleus, formed when a uranium-238 nucleus captures a neutron, has a half-life of 23.5 minutes. By emitting a β particle it then forms neptunium-239 with a half life of 2.35 days. Neptunium-239, in turn,

while they envelop an enormous amount of energy, they release that energy only when they are exposed to extremely high temperature (another form of energy).[88]

Figure 16

In terms of a human power complex all depends on the cohesion of its components and how much of its energy it has to expend to hold itself together and mobilize itself and how much of its

---

emits a ß particle and converts itself into a plutonium-239 nucleus which can last over 24.360 years. Miner, 1964.

88. Known in physical science as the thermonuclear reaction which takes place by the fusion of the hydrogen (deuterium and/or tritium) atom.

VII. Spheres of Power

energy it can generate as a power complex. The proposition reverts back to our earlier discussions, from the nature of the product to the coefficients of power. Using different dynamics discussed in this chapter, a power complex may circumscribe its sphere in order to enhance the sensation or illusion of power within. We are referring to a gamut of situations from the exclusivity of clubs or study groups to development of jargons by professions, or economic protectionist policies by a country.

The circumscription can be used as a vehicle for internal dynamics and cohesion and to create an identity for the sphere making its penetration by the components of other power complexes more difficult. Rules of the game, so to speak, develop. Different sources of power evolve in particular ways and gain different weights creating specific social patterns. In some cultures title and pedigree (reputation) may become the weightier source of power, in another money (means), and in yet another different combinations of networking and connections. In any of these variations, of course, consciousness of power and the capacity to effectively analyze, evaluate and act will give the edge to the power seeker. But the prevalent and prescribed patterns of behavior can condition that capacity, *i. e.*, in different cultures consciousness and analytical qualities are sharpened towards acquiring title, wealth or connections.

Circumscription of the sphere may make the power complex itself less agile in penetrating other power complexes. The name of the game in the United States may not be the same as in France. A successful American power complex may not be able to operate as successfully within the French environment. All this again depends on the adaptability of a power complex, and the potentials it has bottled up within its sphere. When Commodore Perry dropped anchor in Edo Bay in 1853, Japan was a power complex enclosed unto itself. The history of Japan since then provides a graphic illustration of the dynamics of the sources and spheres of power covered so far.

VIII

RESISTANTS OF POWER

In the social setting, when the dominant and the dominated components of a power complex are absolutely integrated in their relational circuit, the totality that ensues should be taken into account as one power entity. It is like a healthy body in which the kidney and the nose have coordinated functions within the whole and do not exercise power over each other. To become a reality of power, that body, as a potentio-kinetic entity, should come into contact with its environment, *i.e.*, spheres of other powers. In a vacuum, in terms of dynamics of power, it is as good as nonexistent. As we saw earlier, power is a relationship. It involves the domineering and the submitting or contesting factors.

Even in the personal power relationship between parents and the child, what remains outside that particular complex creates other power relations. Beyond the limitations and permissions of the parent-child relationship, the child fits into other environmental situations. His relationships with other children or his imaginary domination over his toys or his pet create within him attitudes often influencing his behavior in the parent-child power complex.

The very unknown and undominated surroundings of an isolated ruler and his subjects are factors which may influence and limit his power complex and the behavior of his subjects who, in one way or another, make use of the surroundings. But these are extreme examples. In the societal context power complexes operate in promiscuity. They often overlap and interpenetrate each other and in their spherical dynamics come into conflict, cohabitation or cooperation. Vacuums do not remain vacuums. When the United Kingdom, in order to compress its area of control after the components of its power had thinned out, announced its withdrawal from the east of the Suez Canal, the expanding U.S., U.S.S.R., and other local powers prepared to take over. One of the consequences was the emergence of Iran as a regional power with its own internal contradictions which eventually gave rise to Islamic fundamentalism energizing, in turn, other power complexes. There exists thus a spectrum of endogenous and exogenous dynamics for power complexes in time and space.

In the struggle for domination and power, the hierarchy of the components of the power complex does not organize itself without clashes, gropings, repeated encounters, perseverances, and challenges.

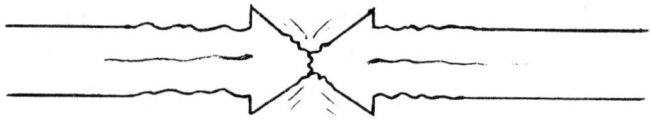

Figure 17

Clashes may cause the contenders to keep aloof from each other, in which case it may be said that no power relationship is established between those particular contenders.

VIII. Resistants of Power

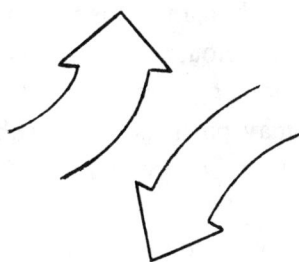

Figure 18

The power that can be generated will depend on the combination of the contending factors and the extent and shape in which they fuse and amalgamate.

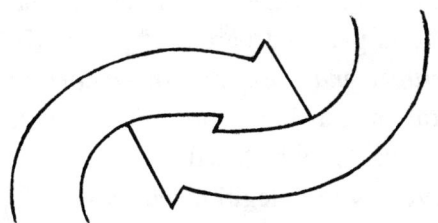

Figure 19

There will, at once, be the centripetal gravitation for active contact and engagement, and centrifugal tendency for freedom, escape and possible attraction to other contenders.

As we proceed in this discussion of the relational nature of power, the implication seems to be that power cannot be conceived alone. In its relativity it needs at least two components:

power and its antimony. In human terms the consciousness of power will tend to call for the consciousness of the elements over which it has power. What is the power which is not challenged? In the manner of Caligula, power may push its docile subjects to the brink of revolt in order to feel their resistance and thus feel itself.[89]

Power, then, is conditional to resistance to such an extent that it cannot be conceived without it: ($P \equiv R$). It follows that there will be degrees of externality and internality of resistance in relation to power such that in the absence of relatively external challenge, the substantiation of power ferments resistants within. Indeed, intrinsic resistants do not ferment only when the comparatively foreign challenge has ceased. Their germs are ever present within the power complex so that in the potentio-kinetic sense power does not cease to exist. This existential relational nature of power implies that resistance is part and parcel of power ($P \supset R$). Lord Acton's *"Power corrupts and absolute power corrupts absolutely,"* was not only a moral maxim but a precept for good government, empirically conceptualizable, which led him to emphasize the need for an opposition even within legitimized power.[90] This janus characteristic of power evokes the dyad of man's existence with which we started our study. The drive for domination emanates

---

89. Game-theory experiments have shown for example, that in a two-person zero-sum game with saddle point, the subjects who figured out the saddle point persisted in taking risks and losing in order to alleviate boredom and "to make the game interesting" (Lieberman, 1960). In another game experiment it was observed that participants considered competing and conquering the opponent to be more significant than cooperating with the opponent for the purpose of lucrative gain. (Minas et. al., 1960).

90. For different views on the social aspects of resistance see the discussion of "contestability", *e.g.*, by Connolly, 1974; MacDonald, 1976; and Lukes, 1977.

from man's dilemma: to be or not to be. It seems, at least through man's vision and understanding of the phenomena, that this is not confined to man but is the law of nature. In physics, at the sub-atomic level, when energy turns into matter, it does so in pairs: an atomic particle (electron) and the symmetric antiparticle (positron). At the other end of the scale we now seem to discover that our universe and its constellations are contained in their infinity by the dyad of matter and anti-matter. Spin the two arrows in our Figure 19 and what you get will not be far from a celestial constellation.

Spiral Nebula in the Constellation Virgo.
Photographed by Mt. Wilson and Palomar Observatories.
Figure 20

And gazing into the skies and fearing and searching the unknown beyond his grasp, which gives him light and darkness, heat and cold, and life and death, man has perceived power in the elements and conceived it in human terms. The magnanimous and mean streaks of the Greek and Aztec gods, the Zoroasterian Ahurmazda and Ahriman, Nirvana (being and nothingness, affirmation and negation), and Ying and Yang in Eastern religions, God and Satan in the Judeo-Christian religions are all manifestations of the dyadic nature of power.

Figure 21

The dyadic conception of the supernatural power does not only arise from man's perception but also from his consciousness about the coefficients of power and its intrinsic resistants. By injecting them into his idea of the holy he can at once expect (and indeed demand) the supernatural to accomplish miracles -- because of the coefficients -- and negotiate with it -- because of the intrinsic resistants: as supernatural powers settle their accounts within, man can take sides and bargain and explain his non-conformity with certain wishes of the gods.

The observation leads us to a fact of much greater significance for our inquiry. It is that not all men gazing into the sky or in awe of the mystery of creation come up with an explanation. Those who do have an edge on the others. Remember, the power of the totem accrues to the shaman. What is pertinent to our study is that those who claim knowledge of the mysteries of heaven use the power of the supernatural to legitimize their own power -- and that of others (the divine right of kings) -- into authority. We thus reach the point of power/authority conversion. While, as we have seen, power cannot be confined to its human perception, authority is man-made. Making the distinction between the two is crucial for our understanding of social phenomena and political organizations. We take the liberty of a short incursion into the conversion of power into authority to underscore this point.

IX

FROM POWER TO LAW AND AUTHORITY

Man's central dilemma in the potentio-kinetic context of power remains the fact that whether in a situation of clash between contesting powers or in that of dominant and dominated elements, the subservient constantly feels the pressure of the powerholders and the latter need to incessantly exercise their power in order to affirm it.

We don't know about the existence of consciousness in supernovas, collapsars, electrons and positrons but, within time and space, human consciousness soon realizes the lack of security in this two dimensional nature of power both for those who submit to power and those who exercise it.[91]

TEMPORAL AND COEXISTENTIAL PHENOMENA

The *temporal continuum* leads to the observation of recurrences and the accumulation of experience: In the long run, the contested powers harden, become breakable or erode, and are overtaken

---
91.   As new scientific discoveries blur the lines of separation between *anima* and *materia*, the study of consciousness about hierarchy and power could gain by observation of other species; starting with the obvious consciousness of primates and going down the line. See, notably, works by Wilson, 1975 (especially the chapter on domination), Griffin, 1984; de Waal, 1989; and Cheney and Seyfarth, 1990.

by others. Looking into the past, present powers may seek ways of securing their own power, and also, creating conditions which make submission, if and when it befalls them, more bearable. The more recurrent the power shifts, the greater the likelihood of powers' consciousness of the need for stability.

The spatial factor is the *coexistential reality* of power: the inevitable coexistence of clashing powers and the unavoidable friction between the superior and the subordinate. The co-existential reality, in the context of the temporal continuum, soon leads to the realization of the need for accommodation. The powers that accommodate create bonds, bounds and servitudes for themselves. In other words, part of their power is transformed into an authority which sets standards upon them for the sake of order, stability and predictability. The proposition hinges on responsibility and accountability. Power does not have to justify its actions -- more on justification later. Authority is answerable and has to respond to someone or some institution which may not necessarily be the subordinate, and/or it may have to behave in some prescribed way. So, in addition to the two dimensions of command and compliance (or clash), arises a third dimension of interaction calling for responsibility.

As we noted at the beginning of this inquiry, it is at the international level, at the point of encounter of autonomous and alien entities, that the distinction between power and authority can best be demonstrated. International law has authority to the extent that those submitting to it recognize it: *pacta sunt servanda*. In the absence of a coercive power above the will of sovereign states, the confronting powers recognize an area of accommodation where they create an authority binding them. They do so to the extent they perceive the temporal/coexistential phenomena. (Figure 22).

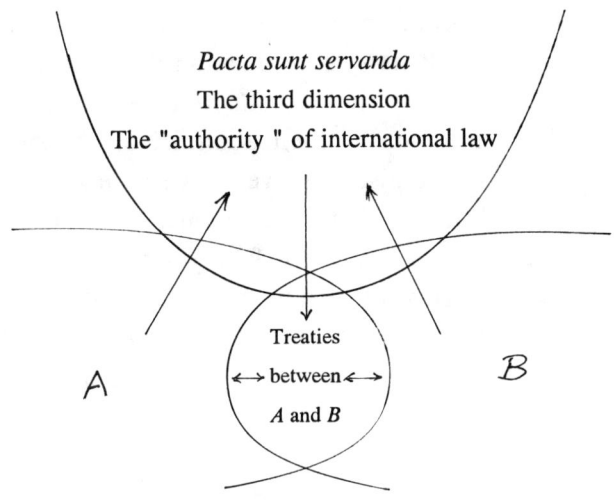

Figure 22

The autonomy and distinctiveness of states account, to a large extent, for the rather precarious nature of international law. Because the powers that be do not identify with enough time series of rise and fall of powers to conclude that in the long run yielding part of their power to a normative system could contribute to the stability of their relations with each other and the security for the exercise of that portion of their power they have retained. Indeed, where interdependence increases and spatial distances are reduced due to development of communications, and where past experiences are identified with by those involved, the chances for the conversion of the power of the states into authority become greater, as has been the case with the European Community. But such instances have been rare in the history of international relations.

In closely-knit small human communities, the temporal and coexistential phenomena -- accumulation of experiences and observation of recurrences within the collectivity -- are close at hand. Recall our earlier discussion of domination drive. As the individual drives for domination, he also observes -- very close at hand -- the growth, potency and decay of other individuals: his parents, himself and his offsprings. Thus, into the family, the clan and the community soon seep norms of conduct: honor thy father and thy mother; love and respect. As Hegel put it, the immediacy of a child's potential freedom are mediated through education into ethical principles.[92]

NATURAL, RATIONAL AND NORMAL BEHAVIOR

To provide continuity, stability and predictability within a community, norms of conduct create bonds and put bounds on the natural inclinations and self-centered rationales of the individual. The natural inclination of a person in heat may be to rape another person. The rational selfish behavior of a hungry man would be to grab the food of a weaker person. The natural inclinations can lead to brute force; the rational calculations, free from norms, can result in unscrupulous use of power. Norms restrain and constrain raw exercises of power. They develop as the natural and rational potentials of man are conditioned by the temporal/coexistential realities. In the last analysis norms have some natural and rational bases. The logic of "thou shall not kill" is that you don't kill and others don't kill you.

---
92.   Hegel, p. 117.

IX. From Power to Law and Authority

But temporal and coexistential phenomena may obscure the original natural and rational bases and substitute them as the sources of the norms. A person will behave in a given way because it is normal; normal because others have behaved and are behaving that way. In some instances the natural and rational bases may no longer apply but the traditional (temporal) and collective (coexistential) realities maintain the norms and mores. Eating pork may have been proscribed in Judaism because of the observation that it could cause trichinosis. Modern hygiene has removed the cause but not the practice.

A normative system of right and wrong, good and bad, allowed and forbidden thus emerges which finds its justification in the collective stability and the predictability it provides.[93] One begins to do or not do as others have done and do, or have not done and do not do. The justification of the binding precepts are temporal and collective phenomena. Here we have the primary elements of 1) *law*: the binding nature of norms; 2) *justice*: the justification of the norms, and; 3) *tradition*: the confluence of the temporal and collective phenomena. The proposition covers the evolution of microcosmic clashes and cooperations among members of families and clans into mores and morality over time within homogeneous communal settings.

The spectrum of conversion of power into law and authority thus extends from the development of moral norms within a community at one end to the development of international law among states at the other end. Between the two, in differentiated social structures, the conversion of power into authority takes a few

---
93.   Khoshkish 1974.

more twists in the relationship between the dominant and the dominated in order to make it possible for some within the society to take certain liberties that others cannot take.

To enjoy their power with stability and with little use of coercion, powerholders should justify their domineering position and the discrepancy between what they can do and others cannot. Above all, that justification should be accepted by those they dominate and those who may contest their power. In a nutshell, to take liberties, power uses coercion while authority uses justification. Nutshells, of course, deform and banalize. The conversion of power into authority is the feat of human social organization: turning power into law to legitimize power into authority in order to exercise power legitimately. (Figure 23).

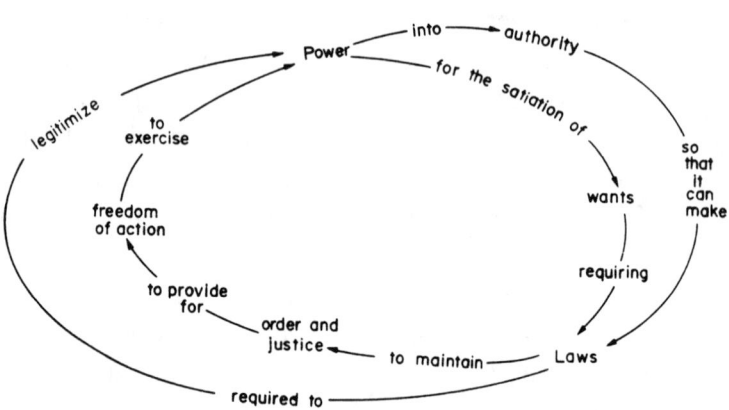

Figure 23

IX. From Power to Law and Authority

LEGITIMIZATION PROCESSES

As the loops in Figure 23 show, it takes power to create authority. Between the two dominant and dominated dimensions of the power complex, legitimization arises as a third dimension binding the two together. It permits the transformation of the lieutenants of the conqueror into the sheriffs of the prince.

For this conversion, what power has to work with and against are its inherent coefficients and resistants. It is the balancing and compromising of the two that produces the legitimizing dimensions. The stronger the coefficients, the more overwhelmed the resistants and the more arbitrary the laws. Cases in point are periods of rule by charismatic leaders and certain periods in revolutions; the coefficient being popular enthusiasm, terror or popular hysteria. In such cases the legitimizing dimension can be rather thin and when the coefficient subsides the authority system has to stand the test of time.

Of course, in historical terms, the move from the exercise of power to its legitimization into authority is not a constant progression. Where authority is challenged by new powers or itself slips beyond the value system which legitimizes it, the need for new dynamics of conversion arises. Thus, for example, as a reaction to the tyrants of sixth century B.C. the ideas of democracy, rule of law and constitutional government were developed by Greek statesmen and philosophers like Pericles, Socrates, Plato and Aristotle; and the Reformation, the religious wars and the emergence of absolute monarchies in Europe gave rise to significant religious, philosophical and literary debates on the legitimacy of power.[94]

The processes and methods of legitimizing power into authority are easier to identify when the coefficients and the resistants are mediated and compromised by the domineering and the dominated within a common value system, such as the rule of a Christian monarch over a Christian population both believing in the divine right of kings. We have identified elsewhere the two main legitimizing processes as *consecration* and *constitutionalization*.[95] In consecration the legitimizing dimension is derived from beyond the power complex itself, either the *supernatural* -- such as the divine right of kings -- or the *traditional* -- rooted in times past. In constitutionalization legitimization is mediated within the power complex and its venues are *contractual* -- drawing on theories of social contract -- and *representational* -- based on concepts of voting, elections and majority rule. We need not elaborate on these processes here and refer the reader to the earlier writing.[96] What is of interest to our present study of the conversion of power into authority is that each process of legitimization runs within a spectrum, at one end closer to power, at the other, to authority.

It is not so much the adherence of the powerful to the process which determines where within the spectrum a regime should be placed, but how effective is the value system on which it is

---

94. Notably, Luther, 1523; Calvin, 1536; "Brutus" 1579; Bodin, 1579; Grotius, 1625; Hobbes, 1647, 1651; Harrington, 1656; Spinoza, 1670; Bossuet, 1679; La Bruyère, 1688; Locke, 1689; Fénelon, 1699; Montesquieu, 1721, 1734, 1748; Voltaire, 1734, etc.

95. Khoshkish, 1979.

96. *ibid.*, ch.11.

based. The Christian king may not only believe in the divine right of kings but may also be a very pious Christian. The president of the republic may be properly elected. But both the king's and the president's authority will depend on how coherently the whole polity upholds the value system on which their authority is based. Ion Iliescu received 85% of the votes for the presidency of Rumania is 1990, yet he had to call on coercive elements to claim his authority, while François Mitterrand, who was elected with 53% of the votes to the presidency of France in 1988, has had little crisis of authority. At issue is the justification of the third dimension -- the legitimizing dimension -- and whether the dominated believe it is imbued with justice.

JUSTIFICATION = JUSTICE

To make the point, let us take, for example, the traditional process of conversion of power into authority where legitimization is based on the temporal/coexistential phenomena. We noted earlier that it served effectively to develop moral norms within homogeneous communities. When applied in a differentiated heterogeneous society, the process reveals Austinian characteristics. That is, as John Austin put it, the authority system is effective when *"the bulk of the given society are in a habit of obedience or submission to a determinate and common superior."*[97] The "bulk," the "habit" and the "determinate and common superior" imply the traditional continuum. Yet, the proposition can work where the differentiation between the liberties of the superiors and the norms imposed

---
97.   Austin, Lecture VI.

on their subjects is not glaring.[98] Without any other justification than "because others have done it that way", great discrepancies can become questionable. Failing justification, the "authority" will have to resort to coercion. Indeed, Austin's description of positive law is based on the habit of obedience and the fear of punishment.[99]

In this traditional model we are presented with a spectrum with, at one end a communal setting with little differentiation and its norms justified by their resilience and, at the other end, an authority with differentiated norms and great propensity to be based on coercion.[100]

The spectrum of coercion/justification evokes the utilitarian and behaviorist concepts of pain and pleasure, and punishment and reward; yet it should not be confused with them. Ours takes off, in part, from our earlier discussion of persuasion as a component of power. There is an element of persuasion in the conversion of power into authority. Part of power's persuasive coefficient is used for legitimization, compromising the power in a value system binding upon it as well. The value system will, of course, present a hierarchy in the norms of conduct in favor of the powerful. The

---

98. Austin points out: *"But the governed, collectively or in mass, are also the superior of the monarch: who is checked in the abuse of his might by his fear of exciting their anger; and of arousing to active resistance the might which slumbers in the multitude."* Austin, Lecture I.

99. Austin, Lecture I.

100. It is because of these contingencies that traditional models are seldom the sole dimension by which the coefficient and resistant of power are mediated into authority. Tradition is usually the buttress of other dimensions: consecration, as in the divine right of kings, or constitutionalization as in a constitutional monarchy.

IX. From Power to Law and Authority

more those subject to the power believe in the righteousness and justice of the value system, both legal and social, the more effective it becomes as a legitimizing factor, justifying the discrepancies. When the accused, as a Sûdra, believes that he deserves the punishment of the king which purifies him for his next reincarnation and his peers think so too, we have a system of authority whose laws are found to be just by those who submit to it.[101] Here we are, of course, dealing with valuational content of justice. The example of the Sûdra should not imply that the totalitarian justification of power should necessarily rest on superstitious grounds. In the Moscow trials of the 1930's many of those accused of treason by Stalin confessed to their crimes against communism, despite being devoted communists -- and because of it. According to some accounts, which are now being substantiated, they did so because dialectically they were convinced that their confession would maintain the legality of their ideology.[102]

Within a differentiated heterogeneous society where different value systems cohabit and compete to serve as bases for righteousness, those who do not find certain laws just in the valuational sense may submit to the broad authority system to preserve the civil society. The concept of *nolo contendere*, besides its common interpretation of non-admission of guilt, implies that the accused does not contest the facts of the case and submits to the court's ver-

---

101.   See, for example, paragraphs 318 and 374 of *The Laws of Manu*, pp.309 & 319.

102.   In *Darkness at Noon*, Arthur Koestler masterfully depicts the dialectical conviction of the accused Rubachev (very much resembling Bukharin, whose confessions and last plea in 1938 were eloquent examples of the point made here). Recent rehabilitations by the Soviet government and statements made by the families of the victims support the scenarios developed by Koestler.

dict although he considers that his action should not have been illegal. He may do so because he may believe that, despite the injustice of the particular law, due process has been applied and it is in his -- and the common -- interest to have the legal institutions respected. While his interest in having the legal institutions respected may imply his belonging to the weightier part of the society -- the domineering elements -- his consideration of the due process evokes the principle of fairness in our equation of justification and justice.[103]

The fairness characteristics of justice are present within our spectrum of coercive power and just authority. At some points within the spectrum, in a differentiated heterogeneous power complex, when value systems are at odds, due process and strict observance of the law may become the minimal fabric of social cohesion. As Barry puts it *"the more a society is divided on substantive values, the more precious as a means of preserving social peace is any agreement that can be reached on the procedure."*[104]

On our spectrum, Barry's proposition approaches the adherence of sovereign states to international law. Even at the international level there are gradations within the coercion/justification spectrum. States carve out of their sphere of power certain areas of law and authority corresponding to different degrees of justification or coercion. The development of Western international law, for example, was steeped in the evolution of the rights of Christian sovereigns. Where a common value system is more or less ap-

---

103.   Rawls, 1958.

104.   Barry, 1965, p. 106.

plicable, it is evoked to buttress agreements. In the absence of common values, the coercive phenomenon becomes more operative and powers keep to their pacts as long as there is balance of power. Hence the existence of the debatable *clausula rebus sic stantibus* in international law. Balance includes the perception of the parties about each other's capacity to inflict harm. The retribution may not be outright act of war but hostage-taking by the proxies of one power which may not have the material capacities of the other one but has a value system which puts less emphasis on human life. Such have been, for example, the cases of hostage-taking in the Middle East.

The principle of fairness as formulated by Rawls implies a consciousness on the part of the members of the society about their social rights and duties.[105] It fits into the constitutionalization process for the conversion of power into authority. But in so far as the broad masses are not consciously engaged in cooperative ventures according to agreed upon rules limiting their liberties for the common good, due process can obfuscate questions relating to the justification of laws and authority. Hence the concepts of equity and social justice and debates in legal philosophy about "rights" in the legal sense and "what is Right" in the moral sense. Our concern here is not a debate on what is and what ought to be[106] but their perception by different segments within a power complex.

---

105.   *Op. cit.* See also Rawls, 1972, where he broadens the concept of Justice.

106.   The formation of values were developed elsewhere. See Khoshkish, 1974.

When the tenant who cannot pay the rent willingly leaves the house because he feels that as a retired person the owner needs the income, the tenant finds the owner's right Right. When more and more renters refuse to leave and find the owners to be exploitive landlords, the owner's right is less and less Right to the extent the society sympathizes with the tenants. The more landlords have to call on the police and the courts to evict renters, the more authority is used for contested power. The justice of the peace may be exercising his authority and reach his verdict with due process, but there will be little justice in his verdict in the eyes of the convicts and their sympathizers.

Note, however, that the assumption here is that the legal system supports the established order as the weightier part of the society. The identification of the weightier part of the society by the legal system will, of course, depend on the value systems present. Where the legal system is directly an issue of the legitimized power and answerable to it alone, it becomes part and parcel of it. Such are, for example, cases of theocratic and totalitarian regimes. Under such regimes, the perception of justice is closely related to the justification of the privileges of the weightier part of the society by the prevailing value system. In 1990, squatters in Moscow occupied apartments which were built for the communist party officials who could once justify their own special treatment by the heavy burden they had assumed to lead the proletariat to the classless utopia.

But where the legal system is relatively independent of the coercive structures, it may become sensitive to weight shifts within the society. Such has been, for example, the evolution of the common law. There is also the case of religious systems dispensing laws, with the belief serving as the legitimizing dimension of monar-

IX. From Power to Law and Authority

chies, and in return the monarchs upholding and propagating the spiritual authority of the religious system; the two serving as checks and balances to each other.

The dependence of different powers on each other for the legitimization process is indeed the measure of justice and justification of authority. One of the causes of the Reformation was that more and more Christians -- including Christian princes -- found the Catholic church's expanding land ownership not Right. Yet, at some point in the history of the Church of Rome, the coefficient of religion had been so overwhelming -- the terror of God so great -- that it justified the donation of land to insure God's ultimate "justice".

There will be the powerful who will have the law on their side and may find it *just* as it is. In the heterogeneous social context chances are that there will always be some who contest the justice of certain laws. Depending on their importance, they may cause social disruption or they may remain marginal to the power/authority conversion system which may otherwise have a broad base of justification. Within the spectrum going from coercion to justification, the legitimate power, authority and the legal system can thus be located at different points. At one extreme, laws can become the coercive tools of power with an appearance of authority, at the other extreme, in a homogeneous community or a monolithic belief system, they can be immersed in moral codes binding the whole together, with patterns of behavior inside each member and little apparent outside coercive body -- as in the case of Hutterite communes mentioned earlier.

It would not be only a *jeu de mòts* to say that, at least in the Western civilization, the words law and justice carry in their origins the concepts developed here. *Lex*, the Latin origin of the word law is derived from *legere* which means bringing together. Justice is derived from *jus* which also means juice and broth. For those who began conceiving these social phenomena, law constituted the ligaments binding the members of the society together while justice lubricated those ligaments. The more there is justification, justice and juice within the body politic, the society and the organism, the less dry and squeaky will be the ligaments and the laws.

X

CONCLUSION

In our incursion into the conversion of power into authority we have trespassed into the domain of legal philosophy. Continuing our research in that context can deviate our attention from the premises we have already established in the distinction between power and authority. Indeed, one of the difficulties in identifying social power is its propensity to flow into other social dimensions, whether law, economy or religion, and to confuse with them. Yet, it is important to distinguish between power and authority, because while power seeks security for its power through legitimization into authority, authority has an endemic tendency towards power. It is that the dulled coefficients and tamed resistants cease to be stimulants. While authority addresses man's needs for security, order and predictability, power tantalizes his cravings for challenge, game and adventure.

We began this inquiry by an attempt to formulate power relationships. But as our reflections on power continued, more variables emerged. Such were the relationships between the product and the goal, the comparative evaluation of different sources of power, the solidity or precariousness of a power complex depending on the shifts in its sphere of power, the coefficients and resistants of power and their use in creating the legitimizing dimension for the conversion of power into authority, the temporal and coexistential phenomena which condition power and develop norms which, in turn, are used both for the control and the exercise of power, the interrelated spectra of coercion/justification and law/justice and their role in distinguishing between power and authority.

For the measurement of these variables we would need multidimensional matrices and complex quantification and computation facilities which, as yet, are not available. The essential fact to retain, however, is that while measuring that which is measurable in the study of power, one should not lose sight of those aspects of power which are not within quantitative grasp. The reduction of the phenomenon to its measurable properties can distort the perception and understanding of the phenomenon. As we measure, we should keep the unmeasurable in mind; it can have an effect on our measurements.

Of course, no awe of the unmeasurable aspects of power is implied. The scientist and the philosopher should remain aloof and simply be conscious of them in order to have a better perspective for analysis. The awe of power is for the philosophically uninitiated; both those who submit to it and those who exercise it. The case of the latter is the more ominous and worthy of close observation. It is when the powerful, whether prophets, visionary leaders or dictators, mistake the coefficients of their power for a mystic mission that they become prone to catastrophes. That is a significant manifestation of man's *Vorstellung* of power in heavens beyond. *I go the way that Providence dictates, with the assurance of a sleepwalker"*, said Hitler.

SELECTED BIBLIOGRAPY

Adorno, Theodore, W., Else Fenkel-Brunswik, Daniel J. Levinson and R. Nevitt Sanford, THE AUTHORITARIAN PERSONALITY, New York, Harper, 1950.

Alker, Hayward, Deutsch, Karl W., and Stoetzel, Antoine, (eds), MATHEMATICAL APPROACHES TO POLITICS, San Francisco, Jossey-Bass, 1973.

Arendt, Hannah, THE ORIGINS OF TOTALITARIANISM, New York, Harcourt & Brace, 1951.

-- , ON REVOLUTION, New York, Viking Press, 1963.

-- , ON VIOLENCE, New York, Harcourt, Brace & World, 1970.

Aristotle, THE WORKS OF ARISTOTLE, Edited by W.D. Ross, Oxford, Oxford University Press, 1908.

-- , ARISTOTLE IN TWENTY-THREE VOLUMES, London, William Heinemann, 1968.

-- , THE COMPLETE WORKS OF ARISTOTLE, edited by Jonathan Barnes, Princeton, N.J., Princeton University Press, 1984.

Aron, Raymond, "Macht, Power, Puissance: Prose démocratique ou poésie démoniaque?", in ARCHIVES EUROPEENES DE SOCIOLOGIE, V, 1 (1964), pp.27-51.

-- , POWER, MODERNITY, AND SOCIOLOGY, SELECTED SOCIOLOGICAL WRITINGS, Brookfield, Vt., Gower, 1988.

Ash, Maurice, "An Analysis of Power, with Special References to International Politics," WORLD POLITICS, III, 1951, pp. 218-237.

Austin, John, (1832), THE PROVINCE OF JURISPRUDENCE DETERMINED. New York, B. Franklin, 1970.

Bachrach, Peter, & Baratz, Morton S. "Two Faces of Power," in AMERICAN POLITICAL SCIENCE REVIEW, LVI, 1962, pp. 947-952.

-- -- , "Decisions and non-decision," in AMERICAN POLITICAL SCIENCE REVIEW, LVII, 1963, pp. 632-642.

-- -- , POWER AND POVERTY, New York, Oxford University Press, 1970.

Bacon, Francis, MEDITATIONES SACRAE, 1597, numerous editions.

Baker, Ernest, NIETZSCHE AND TREITSCHKE: THE WORSHIP OF POWER IN MODERN GERMANY, London, Oxford University Press, 1914.

Baldwin, David A., "Money and Power," in JOURNAL OF POLITICS, XXXIII (August 1971), pp. 578-614.

-- , "Power Analysis and World Politics: New Trends versus Old Tendencies", in WORLD POLITICS, XXXI, 2 (January 1979).

Banfield, Edward C., POLITICAL INFLUENCE, New York, Free Press, 1961.

Barry, Brian, POLITICAL ARGUMENT, London, Routledge & Kegan, 1965.

-- , (ed.), POWER AND POLITICAL THEORY: SOME EUROPEAN PERSPECTIVES, London, Wiley, 1976.

Bell, Daniel, "Is there a Ruling Class in America?" in Bell, (ed.), THE END OF IDEOLOGY, New York, Collier, 1962, paperback, rev. ed. pp. 47-74.

Bell, David V. J., POWER, INFLUENCE AND AUTHORITY: AN ESSAY IN POLITICAL LINGUISTICS, New York, Oxford University Press, 1975.

Bendix, Reinhard, "The Mandate to Rule: An Introduction" in SOCIAL FORCES, LV (December 1976), pp. 242-255.

Bergson, Henri, L'EVOLUTION CREATRICE, Paris, Alcan, 1907.

-- , LES DEUX SOURCES DE LA MORALE ET DE LA RELIGION, Paris, Alcan, 1932.

Blair, G.A., "The Meaning of 'Energia' and 'Entelechia' in Aristotle", in INTERNATIONAL PHILOSOPHICAL QUARTERLY, VII, 1967, pp. 110-117.

Blau, Peter, EXCHANGE AND POWER IN SOCIAL LIFE, New York, John Wiley, 1964.

-- , INEQUALITY AND HETEROGENEITY: A PRIMITIVE THEORY OF SOCIAL STRUCTURE, New York, The Free Press, 1977.

Bose, Nirmal Kumar, SELECTIONS FROM GANDHI, Ahmedabad, Navajivan Publishing House, 1948.

Bossuet, Jacques, LA POLITIQUE TIREE DE L'ECRITURE SAINTE, (1679), Paris, Gallimard, 1979

Selected Bibliography

Bradshaw, Alan, "A Critique of Steven Lukes' 'Power: A Radical View'", SOCIOLOGY, X (January 1976), pp. 121-128.

Brentano, Franz Clemens, PSYCHOLOGIE VOM EMPIRISCHEN STANDPUNKT, 1874, 1911, Leipzig, Meiner, 1924 (Vol. I.) 1925 (Vol. II).

"Brutus, Stephen Junius" (pseudonym), VINDICIAE CONTRA TYRANNOS, (1579), see *infra*. J.H. Franklin.

Burns, Tom R., and Buckley, Walter, POWER AND CONTROL: SOCIAL STRUCTURES AND THEIR TRANSFORMATION, London, Sage, 1976.

Calvin, Jean, INSTITUTES OF THE CHRISTIAN RELIGION, (1536), Grand Rapids, Mich., W.B. Eerdmans Pub. Co., 1986.

Canetti, Elias, CROWDS AND POWER (1960), London, Gollancz, 1962.

Cannon, W.B., "Voodoo Death," AMERICAN ANTHROPOLOGY, Vol. 44, 1942, p. 169.

Cartwright, Dorwin, "A Field Theoretical Concept of Power," in D. Cartwright, (ed.), STUDIES IN SOCIAL POWER, Ann Arbor, University of Michigan Press, 1959, pp. 183-220.

-- , "Influence, Leadership, Control," in J. March (ed.) HANDBOOK OF ORGANIZATIONS, Chicago, Rand McNaly, 1965, pp. 1-17.

Centre Aixois de Recherches Anglaises, LE POUVOIR DANS LA LITTERATURE ET LA PENSEE ANGLAISES, Aix, Université de Provence, 1981.

Cheney, Dorothy, and Seyfarth, Robert, HOW MONKEYS SEE THE WORLD: INSIDE THE MIND OF ANOTHER SPECIES, Chicago, University of Chicago Press, 1990.

Churchill, Winston S., THE SECOND WORLD WAR, 6 Vols., Boston, Houghton Mifflin Co., 1949.

Clark, Kenneth B., PATHOS OF POWER, New York, Harper & Row, 1974.

Clements, Fredric E., "Social Origins and Processes Among Plants," in C.A. Murchison (ed.) A HANDBOOK OF SOCIAL PSYCHOLOGY, (1935), New York, Russell & Russell, 1967.

Cline, Ray S., WORLD POWER ASSESSMENT: A CALCULUS OF STRATEGIC DRIFT, Boulder, Colorado, Westview, 1975.

Coleman, James S., POWER AND THE STRUCTURE OF THE SOCIETY, New York, W. W. Norton, 1974.

Connolly, William E., THE TERMS OF POLITICAL DISCOURSE, Lexington, Mass., Heath, 1974, ch. 2.

Coser, Lewis, "The Notion of Power: Theorethical Developments", in Coser and Bernard Rosenberg (eds), SOCIOLOGICAL THEORY: A BOOK OF READINGS, New York, Macmillan, 1976, IVth edition, pp.150-161

Craven, C. Jackson, OUR ATOMIC WORLD, Oak Ridge, Tennessee, U.S. Atomic Energy Commission, 1964.

Dahl, Robert A. "The Concept of Power," in BEHAVIORAL SCIENCE, Vol. 2, 1957, pp. 201-215.

-- , WHO GOVERNS?, New Haven, Yale University Press, 1961.

-- , MODERN POLITICAL ANALYSIS, Englewood Cliffs, Prentice Hall, 1963 and 1970.

-- , PLURALIST DEMOCRACY IN THE UNITED STATES: CONFLICT AND CONSENT, Chicago, Rand McNally & Company, 1967.

-- , "Power," in INTERNATIONAL ENCYCLOPEDIA OF THE SOCIAL SCIENCES, (ed.) L. Stlls. New York, Macmillan and Free Press, 1968. Vol. 12, 405-415.

Debnam, Geoffrey, THE ANALYSIS OF POWER: A REALIST APPROACH, London, Macmillan, 1984.

Derrida, Jacques, L'ECRITURE ET LA DIFFERENCE, Paris, 1967. WRITING AND DIFFERENCE, Chicago, University of Chicago Press, 1978.

-- , OF GRAMMATOLOGY, (1967), Baltimore, Johns Hopkins University Press, 1974 (1976).

Descartes, René, THE PRINCIPLES OF PHILOSOPHY (1644). Numerous editions.

Deutsch, Karl, THE NERVES OF GOVERNMENT. New York, Free Press, 1966.

Doob, Leonard W., PERSONALITY, POWER, AND AUTHORITY: A VIEW FROM THE BEHAVIORAL SCIENCES, Westport, Conn., Greenwood Press, 1983.

Dornbusch, Sanford M., EVALUATION AND THE EXERCISE OF AUTHORITY, San Francisco, Jossey-Base, 1975.

Durkheim, Emile, THE DIVISION OF LABOR IN SOCIETY, (first published in French in 1893), New York, Macmillan, 1933.

-- , THE ELEMENTARY FORMS OF THE RELIGIOUS LIFE, (Published in French in 1912), Glencoe, Ill. Free Press. 1947.

Selected Bibliography

Emerson, A. E., "The Biological Basis of Social Cooperation," in ILLINOIS ACADEMY OF SCIENCE TRANSACTIONS, Vol. 39, 1946.

Emerson, Richard M., "Power-Dependence Relations", AMERICAN SOCIOLOGICAL REVIEW, XXVII (February 1962), pp.31-41.

Entrevès, Alexander Passerin d', THE NOTION OF THE STATE, AN INTRODUCTION TO POLITICAL THEORY. Oxford, Clarendon, 1967.

Fénelon, François, LES AVENTURES DE TELEMAQUE, (1699), numerous editions.

Fogelson, Raymond D., and Adams, Richard N., THE ANTHROPOLOGY OF POWER: ETHNOGRAPHIC STUDIES FROM ASIA, OCEANIA AND THE NEW WORLD, New York, Academic Press, 1977.

Franklin, Julian H., CONSTITUTIONALISM AND RESISTANCE IN THE SIXTEENTH CENTURY: THREE TREATISES BY HOTMAN, BEZA, & MORNAY. New York, Pegasus, 1969.

Frey, Frederick W., "Comment: On Issues and Nonissues in the Study of Power", AMERICAN POLITICAL SCIENCE REVIEW, LXV (Decenber 1971), pp.1081-1101.

French, J.R.P., Jr., "A Formal Theory of Social Power," in PSYCHOLOGICAL REVIEW, Vol. 63, 1956, pp. 181-194.

-- , and Raven, B., "The Basis of Social Power," in D. Cartwright (ed.) STUDIES IN SOCIAL POWER. Ann Arbor, University of Michigan Press, 1959, pp. 150-167.

Friedrich, Carl J., "Authority, Reason and Discretion", in Friedrich (ed.), AUTHORITY, Cambridge, Mass., Harvards University Press, 1958.

Fromm, Eric, ESCAPE FROM FREEDOM, New York, Farrar and Rinehart, 1941.

Galbraith, John Kenneth, THE ANATOMY OF POWER, Boston, Houghton and Mifflin, 1983.

Gamson, William A., "Reputation and Resources in Community Politics," AMERICAN JOURNAL OF SOCIOLOGY, Vol. 72, 1966, pp. 121-131.

-- , William A., POWER AND DISCONTENT. Homewood, Ill., Dorsey Press, 1968.

Gaudemet, J., "Esquisse d'une Sociologie Historique du Pouvoir" in POLITIQUE, July-December 1962.

Gaulle, Charles de, MEMOIRES D'ESPOIR: LE RENOUVEAU 1958 - 1962, Paris, Plon, 1970.

Gilpin, Robert, U.S. POWER AND THE MULTINATIONAL CORPORATIONS, New York, Basic Books, 1975.

Goldhamer, Herbert and Shils, Edward A., "Types of Power and Status," AMERICAN JOURNAL OF SOCIOLOGY, Vol. 45, 1939, pp. 171-182.

Goldman, Alvin I, "Towards a Theory of Social Power", in PHILOSOPHICAL STUDIES, XXIII, 4 (1972), pp. 221-68.

Gray, John N., "On the Contestability of Social and Political Concepts", in POLITICAL THEORY, V (1977), pp. 331-348.

-- , RATIONALITY AND RELATIVISM IN RECENT WORK IN THE THEORY OF POWER, Hull Papers in Politics No. 17, Hull, University of Hull, 1980.

Griffin, Donald R., ANIMAL THINKING, Cambridge, Harvard University Press, 1984.

Grotius, Hugo, DE JURE BELLI AC PACIS, (1625), Washington, Carnegie Institution, 1913.

Gumplowicz, Ludwik, GRUNDRISS DER SOZIOLOGIE, 1885. tr. OUTLINES OF SOCIOLOGY (ed.) Irving L. Horowitz, New York, Paine-Whitman, 1963.

Han Fei Tzu, THE COMPLETE WORKS OF HAN FEI TZU (3rd Century B.C.) English traslation by W.K. Liao, 2 Vol., London, Arthur Probsthain, 1959.

Harlow, H.F. and Zimmermann, R.R., "Affectional Responses in Infant Monkeys," in SCIENCE, Vol. 130, 1959, pp. 421-436.

Harrington, James, THE COMMONWEALTH OF OCEANA, (1656), numerous editions.

-- , THE POLITICAL WORKS OF JAMES HARRINGTON, Cambridge, Cambridge University Press, 1977.

Harsanyi, John C., (a) "Measurement of Social Power, Opportunity Costs and the Theory of Two Person Bargaining Games," in BEHAVIORAL SCIENCE, Vol. 7, 1962, pp. 67-80.

-- , (b) "Measurement of Social Power in n-Person Reciprocal Power Situations," in BEHAVIORAL SCIENCE, Vol. 7, 1962, pp. 81-91.

Hawley, Amos H., HUMAN ECOLOGY: A THEORY OF COMMUNITY STRUCTURE. New York, Ronald Press, 1950.

Hegel, G. W. F., PHILOSOPHY OF RIGHT (1821), English translation by T.M. Knox, Oxford, Oxford University Press, 1967.

Selected Bibliography

Hendrick, I. "The Discussion of the Instinct to Master," in PSYCHOANAL QUARTERLY, Vol. 12, 1943, pp. 561-565.

Hennen, Manfred, AUTORITÄT UND HERSCHAFT, Darmstadt, Wissenschaftliche Buchgesellschaft, 1977.

Hitler, Adolf, MEIN KAMPF, Boston, Houghton Mifflin, 1943, 1971.

Hobbes, Thomas, ELEMENTS OF LAW, NATURAL AND POLITIQUE, 1640, Numerous editions.

-- , DE CIVE, 1647, Numerous editions.

-- , LEVIATHAN, 1651, Numerous editions.

Hofstätter, Peter Robert, GRUPPENDYNAMIK: KRITIK DER MASSENPSYCHOLOGIE, Hamburg, Rowohlt, 1957.

Hook, Sidney, THE HERO IN HISTORY: A STUDY IN LIMITATION AND POSSIBILITY, New York, The Humanities Press, 1943.

Husserl, Edmund, FORMALE UND TRANSZENDENTALE LOGIK. VERSUCH EINER KRITIK DER LOGISCHEN VERNUNFT, Halle a.s., Max Nijmeyer, 1929.

-- , IDEAS, GENERAL INTRODUCTION TO PURE PHENOMENOLOGY, (1913), Trans. W.R. Boyce Gibson. London, George Allen & Unwin Ltd., 1931.

-- , THE IDEA OF PHEMONENOLOGY, The Hague, M. Nijhoff, 1964.

-- , CARTESIAN MEDITATIONS: AN INTRODUCTION TO PHENOMENOLOGY,(1931), The Hague, Martinus Nijhoff, 1960.

Hutschnecker, Arnold A., THE DRIVE FOR POWER, New York, M. Evans, 1974.

Institut International de Philosophie du Droit, LE POUVOIR, 2 Vol., Paris, 1956-57.

Isaac, Jeffrey C., POWER AND MARXIST THEORY: A REALIST VIEW, Ithaca, Cornell University Press, 1987.

Jennings, Kent, COMMUNITY INFLUENTIALS, New York, The Free Press, 1964.

Jouvenel, Bertrand de, DU POUVOIR, HISTOIRE NATURELLE DE SA CROISSANCE, Geneva, Les Editions du Cheval Ailé, 1945.

Kalish, G. K., Milnor, J. W., Nash, J. F., & Nering E. D., "Some Experimental n-person games," in R. M. Thrall, C. H. Coombs, & R. L. Davis (eds.) DECISION PROCESSES, New York, Wiley, 1954.

Karlsson, Georg, "Some Aspects of Power in Small Groups," in Criswell, Joan H.; Solomon, Herbert; and Suppes, Patrick (eds.), MATHEMATICAL METHODS IN SMALL GROUP PROCESSES, Stanford, Stanford University Press, 1962, pp. 193-202.

Kant, Emmanuel, METAPHYSICS OF MORALS (1797), in KANT'S CRITIQUE OF PRACTICAL REASON AND OTHER WORKS, tr. T. K. Abbott, London, Longmans Green, 1889.

Keohane, Robert O., and Nye, Joseph S., POWER AND INTERDEPENDENCE: WORLD POLITICS IN TRANSITION, Boston, Little Brown, 1977.

Khoshkish, A., "The Concept of Values: A Socio-Phenomenological Approach", in THE JOURNAL OF VALUE INQUIRY, VIII (1974).

-- , "Decision-making Within a Communal Setting: A case Study on Hutterite Colonies", in INTERNATIONAL REVIEW OF MODERN SOCIOLOGY, VI (Spring 1976).

-- , THE SOCIO-POLITICAL COMPLEX: AN INTERDISCIPLINARY APPROACH TO POLITICAL LIFE, Oxford, Pergamon Press, 1979.

Knorr, Klaus, THE POWER OF NATIONS: THE POLITICAL ECONOMY OF INTERNATIONAL RELATIONS, New York, Basic Books, 1975.

Koestler, Arthur, DARKNESS AT NOON, (1940), London, The Folio Society, 1980.

Korda, Michael, POWER: HOW TO GET IT, HOW TO USE IT, New York, Random House, 1975.

La Bruyère, Jean de, LES CARACTERES, OU LES MOEURS DE CE SIECLE, (1688-1696). Translated as CHARACTERS, Baltimore, Md., Penguin Books, 1970.

Lane, Robert E. "The Fear of Equality," in THE AMERICAN POLITICAL SCIENCE REVIEW, Vol. 53, 1959, pp. 35-51.

Lapierre, J. W. LE POUVOIR POLITIQUE, Paris, Presses Universitaires de France, 1953.

Larsen, Mogens Trolle (ed.), POWER AND PROPAGANDA: A SYMPOSIUM ON ANCIENT EMPIRES, Copenhagen, Akademisk Forlag, 1979.

Lasswell, Harold D. POLITICS. WHO GETS WHAT, WHEN, HOW, New York, McGraw Hill, 1936.

-- , POWER AND PERSONALITY, New York, W.W. Norton, 1948.

Selected Bibliography

-- , and Kaplan, Abraham, POWER AND SOCIETY, A FRAMEWORK FOR POLITICAL INQUIRY, New Haven, Yale University Press, 1950.

-- , "World Politics and Personal Insecurity," in A STUDY OF POWER, Glencoe, Ill. Free Press, 1950.

Le Bon, Gustave, THE CROWD: A STUDY OF POPULAR MIND, London, Ernest Benn, 1903.

Le Dantec, Félix, L'EGOISME: SEUL BASE DE TOUTE SOCIETE, Paris, Flammarion, 1918.

Lenin, Vladimir Ilych, WHAT IS TO BE DONE (1902), Oxford, Clarendon Press, 1963.

Lieberman, B. A., "Human Behavior in Strictly Determined 3 x 3 matrix game," BEHAVIORAL SCIENCE, Vol. 5, 1960, pp. 317-322.

Lindblom, Charles E., THE POLICY-MAKING PROCESS, New York, Prentice Hall, 1970.

Lipset, Seymour Martin, POLITICAL MAN, Garden City, N.Y.: Doubleday, 1960.

Locke, John, AN ESSAY CONCERNING HUMAN UNDERSTANDING, (1689)(a), Oxford, Clarendon Press, 1975.

-- , TWO TREATIES ON CIVIL GOVERNMENT, (1689)(b), Cambridge, Cambridge University Press, 1988

Luce, R. D. and Adams, E. W., "The Determination of Subjective Characteristic Functions in Games with Misperceived Payoff Functions," in ECONOMETRICA, Vol. 24, 1956, pp. 158-171.

-- , and Raiffa, M., GAMES AND DECISIONS, New York, Wiley, 1957.

Lukes, Steven, POWER: A RADICAL VIEW, London, Macmillan, 1974.

-- , "Reply to Bradshaw", SOCIOLOGY, X (January 1976), pp.127-132.

-- , "Reply to MacDonald", in BRITISH JOURNAL OF POLITICAL SCIENCE, VII (1977), pp. 418-9

-- , "Power and Authority", in Tom Bottomore and Robert Nisbet (eds.), A HISTORY OF SOCIOlOGICAL ANALYSIS, New York, Basic Books, 1978, pp. 633-676.

-- , "On the Relativity of Power", in S. C. Brown (ed.), PHILOSOPHICAL DISPUTES IN THE SOCIAL SCIENCES, Atlantic Highlands, N.J., Humanities, 1979.

-- , "Of Gods and Demons: Habermas and Practical Reason", in John B. Thompson and David Held (eds.), HABERMAS: CRITICAL DEBATES, Cambridge, Mass., MIT Press, 1982.

-- , (ed.), POWER, Oxford, Basil Blackwell, 1986.

Luther, Martin, SECULAR AUTHORITY: TO WHAT EXTENT IT SHOULD BE OBEYED, (1523)

MacDonald, I. K., "Is Power Essentially Contested", in BRITISH JOURNAL OF POLITICAL SCIENCE, VI (1976), pp.380-2.

Machiavelli, Niccolo, THE PRINCE, (1513) 1532, and THE DISCOURSES, New York, Random House, 1950.

MacIver, R. M., THE WEB OF GOVERNMENT, New York, MacMillan, 1947.

MacRae, Duncan and Price, Hugh D., "Scale Positions and 'Power' in the Senate," in BEHAVIORAL SCIENCE, Vol. 4, 1959, pp. 212-218.

Madariaga, Salvador de, DISARMAMENT, New York, Coward-McCann, 1929.

MANU, THE LAWS OF, translated by Georg Bühler in SACRED BOOKS OF THE EAST SERIES edited by Max Müller, Vol. 25 (1886), Delhi, Motilal Banarsidass, 1964.

Mao Zedong, QUOTATIONS FROM CHAIRMAN MAO TSE-TUNG, Peking, Foreign Languages Press, 1966.

-- , "On Protracted War" (1938), in SELECTED MILITARY WRITINGS OF MAO TSE-TUNG, Peking, Foreign Language Press, 1961, pp. 187-266.

March, James G., "An Introduction to the Theory and Measurement of Influence," in AMERICAN POLITICAL SCIENCE REVIEW, Vol. 49, 1955, pp. 431-450.

-- , "Measurement Concepts in the Theory of Influence," in THE JOURNAL OF POLITICS, Vol. 19, No. 2, May 1957, pp. 202-226.

-- , (ed.), HANDBOOK OF ORGANIZATIONS, Chicago, Rand McNally, 1965.

-- , "The Power of Power," in David Easton, ed., VARIETIES OF POLITICAL THEORY, Englewood Cliffs, Prentice-Hall, 1966, pp. 39-70.

Marcus Aurelius (Antoninus), MEDITATIONS (c.170), translated by George Long and edited by James Gutmann, New York, Washington Square Press, 1964.

Selected Bibliography

Martin, Roderick, THE SOCIOLOGY OF POWER, London, Routledge and Kegan Paul, 1977.

Marx, Karl, WORKS, New York, International Publishers, 1975. Notably:

-- , ECONOMIC AND PHILOSOPHIC MANUSCRIPTS OF 1844.

-- & Friederich Engels, THE GERMAN IDEOLOGY, 1845-46.

-- & Friederich Engels, THE COMUNIST MANIFESTO, 1848.

-- , THE EIGHTEENTH BRUMAIRE OF LOUIS BONAPARTE, 1852.

-- , THE CIVIL WAR IN FRANCE, 1871.

May, Rollo, POWER AND INNOCENCE: A SEARCH FOR THE SOURCES OF VIOLENCE, New York, Norton, 1972; London, Fontana, 1976.

McCleland, David C., POWER: THE INNER EXPERIENCE, New York, Irvington Publishers, 1975.

McFarland, Andrew S., POWER AND LEADERSHIP IN PLURALIST SYSTEMS, Stanford, Stanford University Press, 1969.

Merleau-Ponty, Maurice, "A Note on Machiavelli", in SIGNS, Evanston, Northwestern University Press, 1964, pp.211-23.

Merriam, Charles E., POLITICAL POWER, New York, McGraw-Hill, 1934 (Paper edition, Colliers Books, 1964.)

Michels, Robert, POLITICAL PARTIES: A SOCIOLOGICAL STUDY OF THE OLIGARCHICAL TENDENCIES OF MODERN DEMOCRACY (1915), New York, The Free Press, 1962.

Milgram, Stanley, "Some Conditions of Obedience and Disobedience to Authority," in CURRENT STUDIES IN SOCIAL PSYCHOLOGY (eds. Ivan D. Steiner and Martin Fishbein), New York, Holt Rinehart & Winston, 1965, pp. 243-62.

Mills, C. Wright, "The Structure of Power in American Society," in THE BRITISH JOURNAL OF SOCIOLOGY, Vol. 9, March 1958, pp. 29-41.

-- , THE POWER ELITE, New York, Oxford University Press, 1956.

Minas, J. S.; Scodel, A.; Marlowe, D.; and Rawson, H., "Some Descriptive Aspects of Two-person Non-zero Sum Games II," in JOURNAL OF CONFLICT RESOLUTION, Vol. 4, 1960, pp. 193-197.

Miner, William N., PLUTONIUM, Oak Ridge, U.S. Atomic Energy Commission, 1964.

Montesquieu, Charles, DE L'ESPRIT DES LOIS, (1748), Paris, Gallimard, 1951.

Morgenthau, Hans J., POLITICS AMONG NATIONS, THE STRUGGLE FOR POWER AND PEACE, New York, Alfred A. Knopf, 4th edtion, 1967.

Morriss, Peter, POWER: A PHILOSOPHICAL ANALYSIS, Manchester, Manchester University Press, 1987.

Mosca, Gaetano, THE RULING CLASS (1895/1923), New York, McGraw-Hill, 1939.

Nagel, Jack, "Some Questions about the Concept of Power," in BEHAVIORAL SCIENCE, Vol. 13, 1968, pp. 129-137.

-- , THE DESCRIPTIVE ANALYSIS OF POWER, New Haven, Yale University Press, 1975.

Nash, J. F. Jr., "The Bargaining Problem," in ECONOMETRICA, Vol. 21, 1953, pp. 128-140.

Neustadt, Richard E., PRESIDENTIAL POWER, New York, Wiley, 1960.

Neumann, Franz L., "Approaches to the Study of Political Power: A Contribution to the Sociology of Leadership," in POLITICAL SCIENCE QUARTERLY, Vol. 65, 1950, pp. 161-180.

Neumann, J. von, & Morgenstern O., THEORY OF GAMES AND ECONOMIC BEHAVIOR, Princeton, Princeton University Press, 1944.

Nietzsche, Friedrich. Numerous editions, notably by Oscar Levy (ed), THE COMPLETE WORKS OF FRIEDRICH NIETZSCHE, New York, Russell & Russell, 1909-1913, reprinted 1964; see also Walter Kaufmann's translations, New York, Random House -- Vintage Books, 1967 - 1969. Notably:

-- , DAWN (MORGENRÖTE), (1881)

-- , THUS SPAKE ZARATHUSTRA, (1883-1885)

-- , BEYOND GOOD AND EVIL, (1886)

-- , ECCE HOMO, (1888)

--, NIETZSCHE, A SELF PORTRAIT FROM HIS LETTERS, edited and translated by Peter Fuss and Henry Shapiro, Cambridge, Mass., Harvard University Press, 1971

-- , BRIEFWECHSEL: KRITISCHE GESAMTAUSGABE, compiled by Giorgio Colli and Mazzino Montinari, Berlin, New York, de Gruyter, 1975

Selected Bibliography

Nisbet, Robert, TWILIGHT OF AUTHORITY, Oxford, Oxford University Press, 1975

Oppenheim, Felix E., "'Power' Revisited", JOURNAL OF POLITICS, XL (1978).

-- , POLITICAL CONCEPTS: A RECONSTRUCTION, Oxford, Basil Blackwell, 1981.

Pareto, Vilfredo, THE MIND AND SOCIETY (1916), New York, Dover, 1935.

Parsons, Talcott, THE STRUCTURE OF SOCIAL ACTION, New York, McGraw Hill, 1937.

-- , THE SOCIAL SYSTEM, Glencoe, The Free Press, 1951.

-- , "On the Concept of Influence," PUBLIC OPINION QUARTERLY, Vol. 27, Spring, 1963, pp. 37-62.

-- , "Some Reflections on the Place of Force in Social Process," ed. Harry Eckstein, in INTERNAL WAR, New York, The Free Press, 1964, pp. 33-70.

Piaget, Jean, LE JUGEMENT ET LE RAISONNEMENT CHEZ L'ENFANT, Neuchâtel, Delachaux et Niestle, 1967.

Polsby, Nelson W., "Two Strategies of Influence: Choosing A Majority Leader, 1962," in Robert L. Peabody and Nelson W. Polsby, (eds.), NEW PERSPECTIVES ON THE HOUSE OF REPRESENTATIVES, Chicago, Rand McNally, 1963, pp. 237-70.

-- , COMMUNITY POWER AND POLITICAL THEORY, New Haven, Yale University Press, 1963.

Presthus, Robert, MEN AT THE TOP, New York, Oxford University Press, 1964.

Rapoport, Anatol, RIGHTS, GAMES AND DEBATES, Ann Arbor, University of Michigaan Press, 1960.

-- , and Orwant C., "Experimental Games, A Review," in BEHAVIORAL SCIENCE, Vol. 7, 1962, pp. 1-37.

Rawls, John, "Justice as Fairness," in THE PHILOSOPHICAL REVIEW, Vol. 67, 1958, pp. 164-194.

-- , A THEORY OF JUSTICE, Cambridge, Harvard University Press, 1972 (c.1971).

Richter, C.P., "On the Phenomenon of Sudden Death in Animals and Man," in PSYCHOSOMATIC MEDICINE, Vol. 19, 1957, pp. 191-198.

Riker, William H., "Some Ambiguities in the Notion of Power," AMERICAN POLITICAL SCIENCE REVIEW, Vol. 58, 1964, pp. 341-49.

Rosecrance, Richard, Alan Alexandroff Brian Healy and Arthur Stein, POWER, BALANCE OF POWER AND STATUS IN NINETEENTH CENTURY INTERNATIONAL RELATIONS, Beverly Hills, Dage, 1974.

Rousseau, Jean Jacques, SOCIAL CONTRACT (1762), New York, Harper & Row, 1984

Rummel, Rudolph J., "The Dimensions of Conflict Behavior within and between Nations," in GENERAL SYSTEMS YEARBOOK, Vol. 8, 1963, pp. 1-50.

Russell, Bertrand, POWER: A NEW SOCIAL ANALYSIS, London, George Allen and Unwin, ltd., 1938.

Ruyssen, Theodore, "Les Facteurs psychologiques du pouvoir," in LE POUVOIR, Annales de Philosophie politique, Institut International de philosophie Politique, Paris, Presses Universitaires de France, Vol. II, 1956-57, pp. 87-120.

Schelling, Thomas, THE STRATEGY OF CONFLICT, New York, Oxford University Press, 1963.

Schopenhauer, Arthur, THE WORLD AS WILL AND IDEA (1818), tr. R. B. Haldane and J. Kemp (1883), New York, Dolphin, 1961

Shang-Chun (or Wei Yang) to whom is attributed the BOOK OF LORD SHANG, 4th Century B.C., English translation by J.J.L. Duyvendak, London, Arthur Probsthain, 1963.

Shapley, L.S. and Shubik, Martin, "A Method for Evaluating the Distribution of Power in a Committee System," in AMERICAN POLITICAL SCIENCE REVIEW, Vol. 48, 1954, pp. 787-792.

-- , "Simple Games: An Outline of Descriptive Theory," in BEHAVIORAL SCIENCE, Vol. 7, 1962, pp. 59-66.

Simon, Herbert A., MODELS OF MAN: SOCIAL AND RATIONAL, New York, Wiley, 1957.

Slater, Philip E., MICROCOSM, STRUCTURAL, PSYCHOLOGICAL AND RELIGIOUS EVOLUTION IN GROUPS, New York, Wiley, 1966.

Sorel, Georges, REFLECTIONS ON VIOLENCE, (1906), New York, Free Press, 1950.

Sorokin, Pitrim A. & Lunden, W.A., POWER AND MORALITY, WHO SHALL GUARD THE GUARDIANS?, Boston, P. Sargent, 1959.

Selected Bibliography

Spelt, D.K., "The Conditioning of the Human Fetus in Utero," in JOURNAL OF EXPERIMENTAL PSYCHOLOGY, Vol. 38, 1948, pp. 338-346.

Spinoza, Benedictus de, THE COLLECTED WORKS OF SPINOZA, Princeton, N.J., Princeton University Press, 1985. Notably:

-- , TRACTATUS THEOLOGICO-POLITICUS, (1670).

-- , TRACTATUS POLITICUS, (1677a)

-- , ETHICS, (1677b)

Spruill, Charles, POWER PARADIGMS IN THE SOCIAL SCIENCES, Lanham, MD, University Press of America, 1983.

Stothers, Richard, "Collapsars, Infrared Disks and Invisible Secondaries of Massive Binary Systems," in NATURE, Vol. 229, 1971, pp. 180-183.

Thibaut, John W. and Kelley, Harold H., THE SOCIAL PSYCHOLOGY OF GROUPS, New York, Wiley, 1959.

Toynbee, Arnold, THE STUDY OF HISTORY, London, Oxford University Press, 1934.

Treitschke, Heinrich von, POLITICS, lectures from 1863 on - published first in 1897-98. English tr. by Blanche Dugdale and Torben de Bille, Constable and Co., 1916.

-- , HISTORY OF GERMANY IN THE NINETEENTH CENTURY, tr. by Paul Cedar and Eden, London, Jarrold, 1915-1919.

Trogu, Giancristoforo, FENOMENOLOGIA DEL POTERE, Milan, Nuove Edizioni, 1974.

Untermeyer, Louis, MAKERS OF THE MODERN WORLD, New York, Simon and Schuster, 1955.

Voltaire, François Marie Arouet, THE COMPLETE WORKS OF VOLTAIRE, Geneva, Institut et Musée Voltaire, 1968. Notably, LETTRES PHILOSOPHIQUES (1734).

Waal, Frans de, CHIMPANZEE POLITICS, Baltimore, Johns Hopkins University Press, 1989.

Walter, E. V., "Power and Violence," in AMERICAN POLITICAL SCIENCE REVIEW, Vol. 58, 1964, 350-60.

Weber, Max, THE THEORY OF SOCIAL AND ECONOMIC ORGANIZATION, New York, Oxford University Press, 1947.

White, Robert W., "Motivation Reconsidered: The Concept of Competence," in PSYCHOLOGICAL REVIEW, Vol. 66, No. 5, 1959, pp. 297-333.

Wildegren, Örjan, POWER AND INFLUENCE IN SOCIAL RELATIONSHIPS: A CONCEPTUAL ANALYSIS, Uppsala, doctorial dissertation, University of Uppsala, 1977.

Wilson, Edward O., SOCIOBIOLOGY: THE NEW SYNTHESIS, Cambridge, Harvard University Press, 1975.

Wittgenstein, Ludwig, TRACTATUS LOGICO-PHILOSOPHICUS (1921 in ANNALEN DER NATURPHILOSOPHIE), London, Routledge & Kegan Paul, 1961.

Wolfinger, Raymond E., "Reputation and Reality in the Study of Community Power," in AMERICAN SOCIOLOGICAL REVIEW, Vol. 25, 1960, pp. 636-44.

Wrong, Dennis H., POWER: ITS FORMS, BASES AND USES, London, Basil Blackwell, 1979.

Yeltsin, Boris, AGAINST THE GRAIN, New York, Summit Books, 1990. The reference in the Preface to Boris Yeltsin's bent for leadership was inspired by this book.

INDEX

(For Authors not referred to in the text see Selected Bibliography)

Adorno, Theodore W., 11n.
Acton, Lord John E. E., 86
Actuality, Actualization, 3, 3n.
Adams, E. W., 20n.
Adams, Richard N., 59n.
Ambition, 51
Aristotle, 3n., 79, 97
Aron, Raymond, 3n., 37n.
Ash, Maurice, 3n.
Austin, John, 97, 98
Austro-Hungarian Empire, 30
Authority, 1, 2, 37, 41, 42, 44, 51, 52, 60, 61, 76-78, 89, 91-108
Aztec gods, 88

Bachrach, Peter, vii, 35n.
Bacon, Francis, 50
Baldwin, David A., 3n., 31n.
Baratz, Morton S., vii, 35n.
Barry, Brian, 20n., 45n., 102
Bases of power, 35n., see Sources and Spheres of power
Batista, Fulgenico, 77
Bell, David, 45n.
Bergson, Henri, 60
Bismarck, Otto von, 29
Blair, G.A., 3n.
Bose, Nirmal Kumar, 40n.
Bossuet, Jacques, 96n.
Brentano, Franz Clemens, 57
Brezhnev, Leonid I., 52, 74
Brunei, The Sultan of, 76
Bubiyan island, 4n.
Brute force, see Force
"Brutus", 98n.
Bukharin, Nikolai I., 101n.

Caligula, Gaius, 86

Calvin, Jean, 98n.
Canetti, Elias, 60n.
Cannon, W.B., 58n.
Cartwright, Dorwin, 45n.
Catatonic power relationships, 14-17, 21, 22
Charisma, 46-48, 62, 97
Cheney, Dorothy, 48n., 91n.
Cost to -- of -- power, 20-21, 29-31,35
Churchill, Winston S., 38, 42, 49
Clements, Fredric E., 23
Cline, Ray S., 3
Codrington, R. H., 59
Coefficients of power, 53n., 57-63, 81, 88, 89, 97, 100, 105, 107
Coexistential phenomena, 91-95, 99, 107
Commensal power relationships, 17-19, 22, 23, 24, 26
Competition, 51
Conflicting power relationships, 19, 25-27
Connection, as a source of power, 42, 44, 53, 81
Connolly, William E., 86n.
Consciousness, as a source of power, 8n., 16, 20, 47, 49-55, 57, 62, 81, 86, 88, 89, 91, 92, 103
Craven, C. Jackson, 59n.
Cuba, 77
Czechoslovakia, 74, 75

Dahl, Robert A., vii, 1, 2, 5, 35n. 45n., 57
Darwinian survival of the fittest, 10, 52
Decatur, Stephen, 62
Decision making, 3, 47, 74
Derrida, Jacques, 4n.
Descartes, René, 53n.

125

Deutsch, Karl, 54n.
Divergent Power Relationships, 24-25
Domination Drive, ix, 7-11, 51, 68, 86, 94
Durkheim, Emile, 59
Edo Bay, 82
Emerson, A. E., 26n.
Engrossment factor, 60-61
Entelechy, definition of, 3-4n. See also Potentio-kinetic
European Community, 93
Existential nature of power, 5, 29, 59, 63, 86, 92

Fanaticism, 38
Fénelon, François, 98n.
Fogelson, Raymond D., 59n.
Force, 20, 36-39, 40, 41, 44, 47, 53, 66, 74, 75, 94
Fourier, Charles, 78
France, 37n., 72, 81, 99
Franco-Prussian War of 1871, 29
Freedom of Action, 9, 10, 63, 66
Fromm, Eric, 8n., 10n.

Galbraith, John K., 49n.
Gamson, William A., vii, 5n., 31n.
Gandhi, Mohandas K., 40
Gaulle, Charles de, 71
Germany, ix, 29, 49
Glasnost, ix, 75
Goal, 9, 14-26, 40, 41, 54, 57, 107
Goldman, Alvin I., 14n., 20n., 22n.
Gorbachev, 75
Gray, John N., 2n.
Great Britain, 37n., 50
Greek gods, 88
Griffin, Donald R., 91n.
Grotius, Hugo, 98n.
Gumplowicz, Ludwik, 63n.

Haiti, 76
Han Fei Tzu, 63n.
Harlow, H. F., 8n.
Harrington, James, 98n.
Harsanyi, John C., vii, 5, 17-19, 23, 35
Havet, Jacques, viii

Hawley, Amos H., 17, 26
Hegel, G. W. F., 8, 94
Hendrick, I., 7n.
Hitler, Adolf, 61, 108
Hobbes, Thomas, 5, 35, 39, 63n., 98
Hungary, 74, 75
Husserl, Edmund, 1n.
Hutterites, 78, 105

Ideology, ideological, 2, 3, 37, 40, 101
Iliescu, Ion, 99
Influence, 19, 23, 35, 44-46, 47, 53, 59, 62, 75, 83
International law, relations, 2, 3, 62, 71, 92, 93, 95, 102, 103
Iraq, 11, 38
Iran, 39, 60, 77, 84
Isaac, Jeffrey C., vii, 35n.

Japan, 24, 62, 82
Jenghiz Khan, 48
John XXIII, Pope, 74
Jouvenel, Bertrand de, 58n.
Justice=justification, 99, 100-106, 108

Kalish, G. K. et al., 23n.
Kaplan, Abraham, 35n., 41n.
Karlsson, Georg, 11n.
Kant, Emmanuel, 53n.
Kaufmann, Walter, 53n.
Kelley, Harold H., 45n.
Khomeyni, Ayatollah Ruhollah, 39
Khoshkish, A., 65n., 70n., 78n., 95n., 98n., 103n.
Khrushchev, Nikita S., 74
Kinetic power, energy, 4, 15, 30, 31-33, 35, 54. See also Potentio-kinetic.
Knorr, Klaus, 45n.
Koestler, Arthur, 101n.
Korda, Michael, 41n.
Kuwait, 3

La Bruyère, Jean de, 98n.
Lane, Robert E., 10n.
Lapierre, J. W., 58n.
Lasswell, Harold D., 35n., 41n.

Law and Power, 2, 10, 61, 77, 78, 91-106, 107, 108
Le Bon, Gustave, 68
Le Dantec, Félix, 8n.
Legitimization of power, 44, 52, 76, 97-100, 105, 107. See also Authority.
Lenin, Vladimir Ilych, 61n.
Lieberman, B. A., 86n.
Lindblom, Charles E., 67n.
Locke, John, 53n., 98n.
Loyalty, 61-62
Luce, R. D., 20n.
Lukes, Steven, vii, 2n., 35n., 69n., 86n.
Luther, Martin, 98n.

MacDonald, I. K., 86n.
Machiavelli, Niccolo, 51, 63n.
MacIver, R. M., 35n., 41n.
Mackenzie, Margaret, 59n.
Madariaga, Salvador de, 32
Magnanimity, 61
Manu, the laws of, 101n.
Mao Zedong, 32, 61n.
March, James G., vii, 14, 58n.
Marcus Aurelius (Antoninus), 51
Martin, Roderick, vii
Marx, Karl, 78
May, Rollo, 8
Means of power, 5, 31, 32, 35, 39-41, 44, 47, 48, 81, 102
Merriam, Charles E., 1, 62
Minas, J. S. *et al.*, 86n.
Miner, William N., 79n.
Mitterrand, François, 99
Montesquieu, Charles, 37n., 98n.
Morgenthau, Hans J., 3n. 51n.
Morriss, Peter, vii, 45
Moscow, 104
Moscow trials, 101

Nagel, Jack, vii, 1n., 5n., 22n., 35n., 57, 58
Nazi party, 60
Nicaragua, 77
Nietzsche, Friedrich, 52, 53, 63n.
Nirvana, 88
nolo contendere, 101

Norms, normative system, "normal", vii, 2, 3,
    35, 93, 94-96
Nuremberg, 60

Oppenheim, Felix E., vii
Owen, Robert, 78

pacta sunt servanda, 92
Pahlavi, Muhammad Reza Shah, 77
Panama, 76
Parsons, Talcott, 5, 43
Paul VI, Pope, 74
Perestroika, ix, 75
Pericles, 97
Perry, Commodore Matthew Calbraith, 82
Persuasion as source of power, 2, 44-46, 62, 100
Piaget, Jean, 8
Planck, Max, 4, 31
Plato, 97
Polsby, Nelson W., 5n.
Position as a source of power, 5, 13, 21, 32, 37, 41-42, 47, 49, 52, 53, 67, 70, 76, 96
Potentiality, 3
Potentio-kinetic, vii, 4n., 5, 21, 24, 30-31, 33, 38, 45, 46, 48, 54, 55, 83, 86, 91
Product of power relationships, 14-17, 19, 21, 25, 27, 29-31, 44, 54, 55, 57, 81, 97
Proletariat, 40, 94

Rapoport, Anatol, and C. Orwant, 16n.
Rawls, John, 102, 103
rebus sic stantibus, clausula, 103
Reformation, 98, 105
Reputation, 33, 36, 48-49, 53, 68, 81
Resistants of power, ix, 68, 83-90, 97, 98, 107
Richter, C. P., 58n.
Romanovs of Russia, 77
Rothschild, 48
Rumania 99,
Rumaila, 3n.
Russell, Bertrand, 3, 58n.,

Russia, 29, 77
Ruyssen, Theodore, 58n.

Saddam Hossein, 3n., 39
Sagacity, 51
Schelling, Thomas, 3n.
Schwarzkopf, General Norman, 3n.
Schopenhauer, Arthur, 53
Self-confidence, 46-49
Seyfarth, Robert, 48n., 91n.
Shang-Chun, 63n.
Shapley, L.S., 51n.
Slater, Philip, E., 67n.
Socrates, 98
Somosa, Anastasio, 77
Soviet Union, ix, 38, 43, 74, 75, 101
Spelt, D.K. 7n.
Spheres of power, ix, 35, 44, 63, 65-82, 83, 102, 107
Spinoza, Benedictus de, 53n., 98n.
Stalin, Joseph, 74, 101
Stubbornness, 38, 39
Shubik, Martin, 51n.
Sûdra, 101
Suez canal, 84
Symbiotic power relationship, 22-24, 43

Temporal phenomena, 91-94, 95, 99, 107
Thibaut, J. H., 45n.
Tirpitz, German battleship, 38
Tradition, 95, 96, 99, 100
Treitschke, Heinrich von, 63n.
Trogu, Giancristoforo, 3n.

U.S.S.R., 84. See also Soviet Union
United Kingdom, 84. See also Great Britain
United Nations, 39
United States of America, 3n., 37n., 46, 47, 78, 81
Untermeyer, Louis, 5n.

Vienna Congress, 29
Vietnam, 46
Voltaire, François Marie Arouet, 98

Waal, Frans de, 91

Warsaw, Grand Duchy of, 29
Weber, Max, 2n.
Will, will-power, will to power, 16, 17, 32, 49-55, 74, 92
Wisdom, 51
White, Robert W., 7n.
Wilson, Edward O., 91n.
Wittgenstein, Ludwig, 4n.
World War II, 37
Wrong, Dennis H., 5n.

Yeltsin, Boris, ix
Ying and Yang, 88

Zoroasterian Ahurmazda and Ahriman, 88